KW-306-389

WITHDRAWN
FROM
UNIVERSITY OF PLYMOUTH
LIBRARY SERVICES

RESHAPING
EUROPEAN DEFENCE

edited by Trevor Taylor

THE ROYAL INSTITUTE OF
INTERNATIONAL AFFAIRS
International Security Programme

In association with the European Strategy Group

© Royal Institute of International Affairs, 1994

Published in Great Britain in 1994 by the Royal Institute of International Affairs,
Chatham House, 10 St James's Square, London SW1Y 4LE.

Distributed worldwide by The Brookings Institution, 1775 Massachusetts Avenue,
Northwest, Washington, DC 20036-2188, USA.

All rights reserved. No part of this publication may be reproduced, stored in a retrieval
system, or transmitted by any other means without the prior written permission of the
copyright holder. Please direct all inquiries to the publishers.

British Library Cataloguing in Publication Data
A CIP catalogue record for this book is available from the British Library.

ISBN 0 905031 80 6

Text set in Bembo.
Printed and bound in Great Britain by Redwood Books.

UNIVERSITY OF PLYMOUTH

Item No.	900 263425 6
Date	2 8 FEB 1996 Z
Class No.	355·03304 RES
Contl. No.	0905031806

LIBRARY SERVICES

90 0263425 6

RESHAPING
EUROPEAN DEFENCE

The Royal Institute of International Affairs is an independent body which promotes the rigorous study of international questions and does not express opinions of its own. The opinions expressed in this publication are the responsibility of the authors.

CONTENTS

CONTRIBUTORS

JÉRÔME PAOLINI is Chargé de Mission auprès du ministre, Ministre d'Enseignement Supérieur, in Paris. He was previously a researcher at the Institut Français des Relations Internationales in Paris.

JOACHIM ROHDE is a researcher at the Stiftung Wissenschaft und Politik in Ebenhausen specializing in defence equipment and industrial issues.

STEFANO SILVESTRI is an Italian journalist and a researcher at Istituto Affari Internazionali in Rome.

TREVOR TAYLOR is Professor of International Relations at Staffordshire University and an Associate Fellow of the Royal Institute of International Affairs, London, where he was formerly Head of the International Security Programme.

MATHIAS VAN DEN DOEL is a Liberal Member of Parliament in the Netherlands, having previously been a researcher at the Netherlands Instituut voor Internationale Betrekkingen ('Clingendael'), The Hague, and a Dutch army officer.

HANS HENNING VON SANDRART is a former German army officer who is now a researcher at the Stiftung Wissenschaft und Politik in Ebenhausen.

FOREWORD

The Maastricht Treaty looks forward to the evolution of a common defence policy for the European Union and possibly a common defence – by which something very like a European Army is implied. As the review of 1996 gets closer, these ambitions will inevitably receive more careful scrutiny. Meanwhile, however, each of the member nations is reshaping its national defence policy and armed forces in reaction to the end of the Cold War. It occurred to the European Strategy Group (ESG), on whose behalf the RIIA is publishing this volume, that it would be useful to examine the extent to which these national processes are complementary, as well as conducive to the synthesizing process envisaged at Maastricht. This study embraces the four major West European military powers and, as a foil, one of the most militarily important smaller nations. The introduction and conclusion offer a provisional comparison of the national processes – it cannot be said that the emerging picture is particularly encouraging to enthusiasts for military integration.

The ESG, of which I am currently Chairman, is funded from private sources. It was established in 1985 to facilitate, coordinate and generate multinational security studies in Western Europe, and brings together senior experts from a variety of disciplines and national research institutions specializing in foreign and defence policy studies. As such, it also constitutes an informal consortium of European institutes. Currently it draws its membership from France, Germany, Italy, the Netherlands and the United Kingdom.

The chapters in this book have been discussed by members of the ESG, which is confident that they will be a valuable contribution to wider debate. They do not, however, constitute a collective judgment and the opinions expressed are those of the individual authors.

September 1994   Laurence Martin, Director, RIIA

ACKNOWLEDGMENTS

The editor is grateful to Professor Sir Laurence Martin and other members of the European Strategy Group for their comments on earlier versions of the text. Considerable credit for the production of the manuscript must go to Emma Matanle of the International Security Programme at Chatham House, who encouraged authors and the editor to complete their work and who word-processed the later versions of the text. Hannah Doe and Margaret May of the Publications Department at Chatham House completed the production with their usual patience, good humour and efficiency. As ever, final responsibility must rest with the authors and editor.

September 1994   Professor Trevor Taylor

I INTRODUCTION

Trevor Taylor

Four West European security problems

The end of the Cold War has left West Europeans with four distinguishable, if interrelated, security problems.

The first is that adequate albeit non-provocative defences need to be maintained against the residual threat from Moscow, which has a conventional and a nuclear dimension.

The conventional dimension has been much reduced since President Gorbachev announced unilateral major force cuts at the United Nations General Assembly in December 1988. The Conventional Forces in Europe (CFE) Treaty, the agreements to withdraw Soviet/Russian forces from East European countries, and the break-up of the Soviet Union have all had a major impact in this regard. The Russian threat became geographically much more distant once the last Russian forces had left Germany on 1 September 1994. Russia remains a formidable nuclear power and it is likely that the destruction of its non-strategic nuclear weapons and its strategic nuclear weapons above the 3,000 warhead ceiling, agreed with the US in June 1992, will not be completed until well into the next century.

The West needs also to decide what defence reconstitution provision it needs to make as insurance against the possibility that Russia might, at some point in the future, once more turn into an intimidatory, aggressive state. It also needs to decide which new countries should be covered by Western security guarantees. Any new NATO members would probably be the first to feel pressure from an aggressive Russia.

Second, after the end of Soviet hegemony, a new system of international relations needs to be promoted in Central and Eastern

Europe which will maximize the importance of cooperation and minimize considerations of power politics and conflictual security relations. It may prove possible to integrate some Central and East European states into the Western security community where the threat and use of force plays no part in interstate relations. It may also prove necessary to seek to contain some conflicts in Central and Eastern Europe to the region, so that minimum damage is done to Western interests. Containment is a clear Western goal in former Yugoslavia.

Third, it is in Western Europe's interest that the world beyond the European continent should be marked by international order and cooperation rather than by disorder and civil and international conflict. Direct and rather more elusive interests are at stake. Clearly Western Europe needs the trade in oil and other vital materials to be conducted peacefully, and that makes the Middle East of particular importance. More generally, West Europeans must develop a consistent view on whether aggression anywhere is a threat to their interests and on whether conflicts in one region are likely to have serious negative consequences elsewhere. Having articulated their interests in international order, West Europeans then need to decide how those interests should best be protected and advanced. The place of West European armed forces in the promotion of those interests is a matter for debate, as are arms and other defence-related exports and the utility of economic sanctions.

Finally, while West Europeans do not wish to see the collapse of the North Atlantic security community, they cannot assume that their existing security community will survive the decline of the threat from Moscow and a reduced US presence, following the disappearance of the external threat. One way to ensure that the security community is sustained is to maintain defence on a coalition basis where states do not feel that they are responsible only for their own national defence. As the 1992 British Defence White Paper argued,

> Our security remains inextricably bound up with that of our
> partners in Europe and the Alliance. It remains a key security
> interest to sustain the present network of multinational Western

cooperation and to avoid any reversion to nationally-driven defence.[1]

Even at the height of the Cold War, defence policies in Western Europe were framed by national governments, but for those states which were NATO members, alliance strategy, political commitments and the multinational force planning process were significant pressures influencing their behaviour and the psychological condition of their decision-makers. The renationalization of defence, should it occur, will begin in the thought processes of politicians and officials, rather than in administrative procedures.

In the absence of a major external threat from Moscow, all NATO members basically have more choice in their defence and security policies. A problem in the future will be to maintain a substantial coordination of their defence policies in the absence of a massive, immediate danger. A challenge for West Europeans may be to maintain coordinated positions even after an American withdrawal from Europe.

Guidance from Rome and Maastricht

Since the end of the Cold War, allied and friendly states have sought to address these issues, in part through multilaterally agreed defence and security measures in several forums. The 1990 Paris Charter and associated Conference on Security and Cooperation in Europe (CSCE) agreements, as well as the North Atlantic Cooperation Council (NACC) and NATO's January 1994 Partnership for Peace initiative, represent important definitions of how the West would like to see cooperation develop in and with the former communist bloc; but of particular significance for this project, which is focused on major Western states, are the following: the new force structure agreed for NATO in 1991; NATO's New Strategic Concept agreed in Rome in November 1991; the Maastricht Treaty and associated WEU Declaration of December

---

1. *Statement on the Defence Estimates*, 1992, Cmnd 1981, London, HMSO, July 1992, p. 8, para. 6.

1991; the Petersberg Declaration of the Western European Union of 19 June 1992; and the conclusions of the Portuguese presidency of the EC published at the end of June 1991 (specifically Annex 1).

NATO's new force structure, to replace the 'layer cake' arrangement which had been used during the Cold War, places a clear emphasis on the undesirability of the renationalization of defence by stressing the role that multinational units should play, especially in NATO's Reaction and Main Defence Forces. The Allied Rapid Reaction Corps (ARRC) was originally envisaged as having divisions from eight countries.

Three queries hang over the force structure as planned to date. One is whether it will appear appropriate once Russian forces have withdrawn from Germany and Poland. Will not NATO appear over-endowed with ill-prepared main defence forces in the centre of Western Europe when real problems are more distant? A second issue is to determine the eventual size of the US commitment. This remains fundamentally uncertain. President Bush talked of 150,000 US troops remaining in Europe, though it seems that 75,000 is likely to be the actual figure within a few years. A third issue is whether having mainly national divisions in multinational corps will have any significant 'psychologically integrating' effects on the soldiers and politicians concerned or whether the national identity of their units will remain of prime importance to them.

NATO's New Strategic Concept demonstrated that the organization could rethink its position in new circumstances but is open to the charge that it does not mark a real break from flexible response, and it is hard to feel confident that the agreed document will necessarily prevent future possible conflicts on nuclear issues. It sends appropriate cooperative messages to Moscow and endorses the contribution which European defence cooperation could make, but it does not in itself provide specific guidance for the future development of national defence policies, nor does it have any capability to ensure that states develop their forces along the broad lines suggested by NATO. The Maastricht Treaty stressed that security and perhaps defence cooperation would become matters for the European Union (EU). In essence it identified the type of world the signatories wanted to see, but gave little guidance as to the means which would be used or the prices which the members were willing to pay to achieve their ends.[2] A document, agreed but not incorporated into the treaty, listed security areas in which EU members aspired to cooperate. These comprised arms control and disarmament, the CSCE, proliferation, and the economic aspects of security including arms exports. This document was noted and endorsed, but not further developed, at Lisbon in June 1992. Overall the Common Foreign and Security Policy (CFSP) aspired to cooperation in all areas 'related to the security of the Union, including the framing of a common defence policy'[3] while not threatening 'the specific character of the security and defence policy of certain Member states'.[4] An ad hoc security working group of the political committee of the European Council was created under the British presidency.

In the WEU Declaration accompanying the Maastricht Treaty, WEU states agreed on 'the need to develop a genuine European security and defence identity and a greater European responsibility on defence matters' and made a commitment that 'WEU will be developed as the defence component of the European Union and as the means to strengthen the European pillar of the Atlantic Alliance. To this end it will formulate common European defence policy.' Members agreed to put in place administrative arrangements to facilitate the coordination of WEU activities with those of NATO and the EC/EU and identified ways of strengthening the WEU's operational role. Since the beginning of 1992, a WEU military planning cell has been established, and schemes for the command and operation of WEU forces have been articulated.[5] Chiefs of Defence Staff have begun to hold twice-yearly meetings. It has been asserted that multinational and

2. See Treaty on European Union, Article J. 1, paras. 2 and 3.
3. Treaty on European Union, Article J. 4, para. 1.
4. Treaty on European Union, Article J.4, para. 4; reiterated in para. 37 of Annex 1 of the 'Conclusions of the Portuguese Presidency', 29 and 30 June 1992.
5. See Admiral Ben Bathurst, speech at the Royal United Services Institute, London, June 1992.

light units might be particularly suitable as forces answerable to the WEU and a study group has been set up to consider the establishment of a European armaments agency. The second section of the Petersberg Declaration, 'on strengthening the WEU's operational role', is reproduced as Appendix 1 to this introduction. The definitions of associate member and observer status of the WEU were also settled at Petersberg.

The Franco-German Corps, now the Eurocorps, was proposed in October 1991 and planned in greater detail after Maastricht. It will be operational by 1995. Questions were raised about its relationship to NATO and WEU structures, although by mid-1992 it was clear that its German units would have an assigned NATO role, that the corps as a whole would contribute to the defence of NATO territory in the event of crisis, and that it would be made available to the WEU planning cell for planning purposes. Although Paris and Bonn stressed that the corps would reinforce the principle and practice of multinationality (10,000 French troops would be stationed in Germany while a number of German officers would be based at the corps headquarters in Strasbourg), there was some suspicion in other parts of Western Europe that the promotion of the corps represented an undesirable bilateral initiative at a time when multinational cooperation through established international organizations was supposedly the preferred way forward. However, the corps later acquired further multinational credentials when Spain and Belgium decided to contribute.

The role and shape of this work

The future could be marked either by a continuation of the degree of defence cooperation traditionally present in NATO, or by the renationalization of defence, or by increased cooperation, even integration, among Europeans. Although NATO has always sought to intensify cooperation among its members, the New Strategic Concept aims essentially at the maintenance of established levels of cooperation, while the EU/WEU developments involve aspirations to much intensified cooperation among European states.

While these multilateral developments have provided a broad framework for direct change in national policies, guidance has not been comprehensive, completely coherent, entirely clear or politically mandatory. Since the late 1980s and the initial improvements in East–West relations, West European governments have been adjusting their national defence policies, either on an incremental basis or through more major reviews.

Thus the central tasks for this project were:

- to seek out compatible and complementary features among the emerging defence and security policies of different states. Compatibility and complementarity need to be viewed in terms of the multilateral commitments referred to above, and also with regard to the national actions of other allies;
- to identify incompatible features in such emerging policies; and
- to make proposals to generate greater harmony and complementarity among national policies.

Five countries, all of them politically and militarily central to the West European defence effort, are featured below in chapters addressing a parallel range of concerns. These chapters, on France, Germany, Italy, the Netherlands and the United Kingdom, produce an information base from which general implications are drawn in the concluding chapter.

To ensure that each national chapter covered the same range of subjects and that different countries could be compared, authors were asked to address defence and security policies through a series of common questions, as follows. Areas (1) to (5) involved the shape and immediate determinants of defence policy. Areas (6) and (7) looked at broader domestic and international environmental pressures.

(1) What basic foreign policy and strategic thinking underpins a state's defence policy, including the expectations of the future US role in Europe which policy reflects? Is it assumed that the

US, in broad terms, will be present in Europe? Alternatively, is defence and security policy being framed so that it can cope with US presence or absence? Moreover, how does a state tend to view its responsibilities in the international order as a whole; with which regions has it a particular concern; what problems does it feel are most serious; and how does it view the utility of military instruments? Information is sought on what sort of state a country feels it could and should be, and what sort of military roles it believes Western Europe should play in the world. In what scenarios, if any, does a government envisage that it might use its armed forces, and what role do scenarios play in guiding defence planning?

A clear possibility is that a government's thinking in these areas may as yet be inchoate and not articulated. Such a situation may offer both obstacles and opportunities regarding the coordination of defence policies.

(2) Defence policy is clearly reflected in planned and actual spending levels, and burden-sharing will be an intra-European as well as a transatlantic issue. Thus information was sought on how much governments currently spend and what they intend to spend in future, both in real terms and as a share of national income. It is also significant to know how the balances of expenditure are to change, especially between equipment and personnel spending. How will budgetary shares among the army, air force and navy change? What does planned expenditure on training say about policy?

(3) How are force structures to change? A range of issues arises here, including how the balance is to develop between volunteer and conscript forces, and between full-time and reservist troops. What is the changing numerical relationship of air, land and naval forces? How many units will be kept at 'full readiness' and how many will take 'a considerable time' to build up to full strength? What is the envisaged balance between light/mobile

forces and heavy armoured units? What provision will be made for specialized forces dealing with peacekeeping, humanitarian relief missions, disaster relief, etc.?

(4) What equipment plans are associated with envisaged force structures? The levels of spending on equipment and of the specific major items to be acquired must be considered. Can it be anticipated that equipment spending will be adequate to generate the desired force structures and levels of capability, including the provision of logistic support? Of related concern is how equipment is to be procured. What use will be made of collaborative projects, of preferred national suppliers, of Europe-wide competition and of the defence industrial base of NATO as a whole? What is a government's attitude towards the continued implementation of Article 223 of the Treaty of Rome? How important are defence industrial considerations in defence policy and what is the nature of any such considerations?

(5) What is the time scale of change and adjustment in defence policy? Is change being planned for a decade, and, if so, of what degree, or do governments feel able to look ahead for only a couple of years? Are defence capabilities being designed which have the clear potential to be strengthened if the international environment deteriorates, or reduced if things go well politi-cally? Do equipment acquisition plans seem compatible with spending?

(6) In adjusting national defence policies, what are the weight and thrust of domestic political considerations? Is there a clear expectation of a substantial peace dividend? How important is defence/security policy perceived to be? How salient are defence employment considerations? What domestic opposition exists to the government's defence plans and how significant is it? Does the government enjoy the support of a large degree of national consensus on defence? Are balanced forces a political necessity, or would a greater degree of force specialization among allies be

acceptable? Can defence 'sacred cows' be identified on such topics as the hosting of foreign forces?

(7) Analysis of the national environment of defence clearly needs to be complemented by an assessment of the weight of the international environment. How seriously has the NATO force planning process been taken in the past and how weighty might multilateral and bilateral external influences be in the future? If little notice of alliance pressures was taken in the past, when the immediate threat was great, can it be expected that the preferences of allies will have much impact in the future, when the immediate threat is much reduced?

Summary

The cooperative commitments made in EU/EC, WEU and NATO frameworks reflect the preference in principle of West European governments that defence should become an area of intensified rather than diminished cooperation. However, national needs continue to be recognized and there are few hard and fast commitments to specific elements of defence integration.

It is thus prudent to examine, through detailed scrutiny of national choices and changes, the compatibility of national policies both with each other and with the multilateral agreements made in the early years of this decade. The chapters which follow, while differing somewhat in their nature, offer valuable insight and data on defence policy changes in these states, which are central to the advance of a more coherent West European defence identity.

APPENDIX: EXTRACT FROM THE PETERSBERG DECLARATION, 19 JUNE 1992

On strengthening WEU's operational role

1. In accordance with the decision contained in the Declaration of the member States of WEU at Maastricht on 10 December 1991 to develop WEU as the defence component of the European Union and as the means to strengthen the European pillar of the Atlantic Alliance, WEU member States have been examining and defining appropriate missions, structures and means covering, in particular, a WEU planning cell and military units answerable to WEU, in order to strengthen WEU's operational role.

2. WEU member States declare that they are prepared to make available military units from the whole spectrum of their conventional armed forces for military tasks conducted under the authority of WEU.

3. Decisions to use military units answerable to WEU will be taken by the WEU Council in accordance with the provisions of the UN Charter. Participation in specific operations will remain a sovereign decision of member States in accordance with national constitutions.

4. Apart from contributing to the common defence in accordance with Article 5 of the Washington Treaty and Article V of the modified Brussels Treaty respectively, military units of WEU member States, acting under the authority of WEU, could be employed for:

   • humanitarian and rescue tasks;
   • peacekeeping tasks;
   • tasks of combat forces in crisis management, including peacemaking.

5. The planning and execution of these tasks will be fully compatible with the military dispositions necessary to ensure the collective defence of all Allies.

6. Military units will be drawn from the forces of WEU member States, including forces with NATO missions – in this case after consultation with NATO – and will be organized on a multinational and multiservice basis.

7. All WEU member States will soon designate which of their military units and headquarters they would be willing to make available to WEU for its various possible tasks. Where multinational formations drawn from the forces of WEU nations already exist or are planned, these units could be made available for use under the authority of WEU, with agreement of all participating nations.

8. WEU member States intend to develop and exercise the appropriate capabilities to enable the deployment of WEU military units by land, sea or air to accomplish these tasks.

9. A Planning Cell will be established on 1 October 1992, subject to practical considerations, under the authority of the Council. It will be located with the Secretariat-General in a suitable building in Brussels. The Council has today appointed Maj. Gen. Caltabiano (Italian Air Force) as its first Director. The Planning Cell will be responsible for:

- preparing contingency plans for the employment [of] forces under WEU auspices;
- preparing recommendations for the necessary command, control and communication arrangements, including standing operating procedures for headquarters which might be selected;
- keeping an updated list of units and combinations of units which might be allocated to WEU for specific operations.

10. The Council of Ministers approved the terms of reference for the Planning Cell.

Source: Agence Europe, *Europe Documents* No. 1787, *Atlantic Document* No.79, 23 June 1979, Section II.

2 THE FRENCH CASE

Jérôme Paolini

It has taken some five years for France to begin to adjust its security policy to the new world emerging from the debris of the Cold War. The attempt, which has taken the form of France's first Defence White Paper in 22 years and preparations for the 1995–2000 defence budget, has occurred in a domestic political setting dominated by the prospect of the 1995 presidential contest, and characterized by the anomaly of 'cohabitation' between a socialist president and a Gaullist/conservative prime minister. It is thus hardly surprising if much of current thinking, including the 1994 Defence White Paper, raises more questions than it resolves.

The legacy of the past

To understand what is at stake in adapting France's defence capabilities to the post-Cold War period, one has to begin with the legacy of the past. This legacy consists, in the first instance, of a conceptual framework which from the time of Charles de Gaulle has been made up of three core beliefs: the permanence and centrality of the nation-state in the international strategic game; the inevitable evolution of European and global security beyond the bipolar confrontation; and, finally, the necessity for the Atlantic alliance to mature into a strategic framework linking Europe and the United States as equals. Until the strategic revolution of 1989–90, this conceptual framework had remained essentially unchanged and continuity was embedded in the will of successive presidents of the Fifth Republic to uphold France's autonomy, sovereignty, independent means and original body of strategic thought. Such continuity allowed successive governments to implement ambitious multi-year military programmes – devoting an average of 3.8 per cent of GNP to defence since the mid-1970s – in effect making France the only medium power still claiming to be a world one, notably because it maintains the type of strategic and power-projection forces required for a global role, and demonstrates the will to use them.

The legacy also consists of hardware – a complex of military forces – and the doctrines and processes for using them, the most important characteristic of which is the primacy afforded to nuclear weapons, at least until very recently. France has created and deployed over three decades a nuclear arsenal that made it into a 'mini-superpower': strategic forces comprising a triad of land, sea and air-launched systems as well as the complete pre-strategic spectrum of land, sea and air-launched tactical weapons. After the gradual build-up of the *force de frappe* in the 1970s and early 1980s, France devoted a growing effort to conventional forces without slackening the pace of nuclear modernization. From this combined procurement effort, achieved though five-year procurement planning laws approved by the parliament, springs the desire for real technological independence and the determination to supply the French armed forces with equipment produced by the French defence industry, ranging from combat aircraft and main battle-tanks to aircraft carriers and, of course, nuclear systems. This goal of national autonomy in defence procurement has resulted over the years in the acquisition of nearly all French weapons from domestic sources or joint ventures involving French companies, even when technologically superior or less expensive alternatives were available abroad. Over the past 30 years, an impressive defence industrial base has been built. But because of the small size of the domestic arms market, concentration at prime-contractor level has led to a group of sole-source, 'national champion' firms which are national repositories of design and manufacturing know-how for entire sectors of defence equipment. The industry also relies heavily on export sales, notably to developing countries, to amortize overhead costs and to permit the economic production of weapons for France's own use.

Questions for the future

Since 1989, however, the strategic revolution launched by the fall of the Berlin Wall has brought these fundamental principles of French defence policy into question. First of all, the likely future course of the former Western bloc beyond the old bipolar system is in itself a challenge. France has played a key role in opening the way, at the Maastricht summit of late 1991, to a European Union eventually leading to a common defence among its members. Much is at stake here for France since a politically and strategically united Europe would demand more military integration than did NATO, which France has always kept at arm's length. By continually stressing the need to transform the WEU into the defence arm of the future European Union and by actually creating a joint multinational 'Eurocorps' with Germany and others, France's defence policy has entered a phase of gradual denationalization in favour of European integration. French policy-makers and defence experts thus frequently offer a clear reminder in the current debate on the risk of renationalization of defence in Western Europe: more European integration should be pursued in the defence realm. The challenge is twofold, touching the core beliefs of French sovereignty and independence. France must, on the one hand, continue to be the prime promoter of the strategic unification of Western Europe, of which it sees the Maastricht Treaty as just a starting point, by proposing concrete initiatives in the areas of defence and security. But, on the other hand, it must also accept the consequences this process will inevitably have, both real and symbolic, for its own strategic independence.

While France has not turned its back on the prospects for a common European defence identity, those prospects have clearly receded since the momentum of European integration was at the very least slowed down by the difficult process of ratifying the Maastricht Treaty (not exclusively in France). In parallel, and partly as a result of this, the past two years have witnessed a reassessment of French policy towards and within NATO. This is a subject for ongoing internal debate and, whereas full absorption into NATO's integrated command structure is almost unanimously rejected, a number of proposals have been made and concrete steps taken. For instance, in December 1992, France decided to take part fully in the NATO Military Committee's discussions on peacekeeping operations. Then, soon after his nomination as Foreign Minister, Alain Juppé stated that the revamping and consolidation of NATO rested upon the emerging reality of European integration, and that the future of NATO had to move from American leadership to transatlantic partnership, with a more active French and European role within the alliance.[1]

Second, emerging instabilities in Eastern Europe made clear from 1990 onwards that the primacy of nuclear weapons in balancing the continent's tensions could only become more doubtful as time went on. While such weapons remain an essential component in France's defence and security policy, most of the theatres of crisis and conflict in Europe (former Yugoslavia, for example) are unlikely to involve France's vital interests and therefore do not justify recourse to the threat of nuclear use. So nuclear weapons have become for France, as they have for the other nuclear weapon states, 'weapons of last resort'. Having invested so much in this field, France has had to reduce the part nuclear weapons play in its defence policy, both in terms of procurement and in its strategic doctrine. As for new regional conflicts around the world with which France must be prepared to deal, the nature of the security problems in the South is not essentially different from those of Eastern Europe, the Balkans or the former Soviet Union: border disputes, confrontations over minorities, and the proliferation of weapons. As a permanent member of the Security Council, France has considerably stepped up its direct contribution to international stability under UN auspices. While it seldom participated in such operations during the Cold War, France became in 1993 the leading net contributor to UN peacekeeping missions with around 10,000 men committed in areas from Cambodia to Somalia and former Yugoslavia. The Gulf war against Iraq in 1990–91 had confirmed that a defence policy resting primarily on nuclear deterrence is hardly suitable for international policing missions. Even if the risks of nuclear proliferation in the South

1. *Le Figaro*, 18 May 1993.

and in the East justify the maintenance of a French nuclear arsenal, the new strategic environment clearly obliges France to refocus its defence efforts in favour of conventional forces and power projection, as the 1994 Defence White Paper stresses.[2]

Finally, these new strategic realities have called into question central assumptions of French defence policy at a time – the late 1980s and early 1990s – corresponding to the end of a 'procurement macrocycle' involving practically all major weapon systems equipping the three services of the French armed forces. Neither the United Kingdom nor Germany or the United States has to face the daunting task of procuring *simultaneously* during the 1990s the following items: a new generation of nuclear aircraft carriers for the navy, a new multi-role combat aircraft (Rafale) for both the air force and the navy, and a new armed attack helicopter and a new main battle-tank (Leclerc) for the army, in addition to replacing all three legs of the strategic nuclear triad. This list mentions only the most important programmes. The procurement bottleneck of the 1990s is the direct consequence of French military spending in the previous two decades. The first three five-year procurement spending plans of the Fifth Republic (1960–75) were almost exclusively devoted to nuclear programmes, after which the next three plans focused on conventional systems. Because of this phased approach, both nuclear and non-nuclear programmes were to reach in conjunction the beginning of their procurement cycle in the early 1990s.

The need for overhaul

By the late 1980s, before the end of the Cold War, it had become evident that a complete overhaul of French defence policy, with major industrial consequences, could not be avoided, since releasing this bottleneck would have needed, in real terms, the procurement level of the 1989 defence budget for 10 years. Such expenditure would only have paid for commitments already entered into for weapons planned or ordered and programmed. No new commitments would have been

2. *Livre blanc sur la défense*, Ch. 5, Sections 3 and 5.

possible. Yet such spending became inconceivable after the downfall of the Soviet Union when defence budgets started their net decline under pressure from economic trends and the country's financial situation.

By early 1990, when the French government initiated the preliminary studies in preparation for the new 1992–6 procurement spending plan, it had become clear that a radical reform of French defence policy was urgently needed. The challenge presented to policy-makers was considerable, since the transformation had to be made in terms of both doctrine and force structure. It had to entail the redefinition of the armed forces' roles and missions and thus France's own role in the world, as well as a thorough restructuring of the forces in three directions: de-emphasizing the reliance on nuclear deterrence in favour of conventional forces; emphasizing smaller, professional units for force projection rather than large, more static central front-oriented conscription forces; and, finally, formulating principles to guide a reshaping of the country's cumbersome national defence industry. Yet, for three essential reasons, these urgent choices were not made quickly.

Factors delaying reform

Politics

First, there was politics. By late 1992, no consensus had emerged, either in government or in the opposition, in favour of clear and convincing policies adequate to the challenge. The exigencies of current domestic politics – particularly the general election of 1993 and the presidential contest of 1995 – were highly unfavourable for a medium- to long-term effort in the defence-planning realm. One of the key politically divisive factors was the problem of conscription. Deeply anchored in French national culture since the Revolution, conscription remains at the crossroads of the debate on national cohesion and national defence. In 1990, the French army numbered some 288,000 men, of whom half were conscripts serving for a 12-month period and, with the exception of a few Foreign Legion regiments, no units were completely professionalized. France's participation in Operation 'Desert Storm' highlighted the difficulties of adapting such an army to new strategic realities. Since Operation 'Daguet' (the French contribution to the Kuwait campaign) was to exclude conscripts, it could barely involve 16,000 professional soldiers out of a total of just over 450,000 in the French armed forces as a whole. Sending a division-size force to free Kuwait was the result of a maximum effort on the part of France and it was still too small, both in comparison with the United Kingdom (which managed to send twice as many soldiers) and in comparison with France's own ambitions. This modest showing in numbers fielded stemmed principally from a fundamental structural problem: conscription.

While national service was appropriate to a military whose primary Cold War vocation was defending the country's vital interests in Germany, conscription is much less compatible, and perhaps incompatible, with collective security missions necessarily involving operations far from home territory. Yet conscription has become a major obstacle, preventing the needed reconfiguration of the French army. Although the Gaullist Rassemblement pour la République (RPR) party, then in opposition, had officially argued in favour of abolishing the draft after the Gulf war, President Mitterrand decided to maintain conscription with a reduction from 12 to 10 months of service. After the general election of March 1993, the victory of the conservative coalition, and the advent of the Fifth Republic's second round of 'cohabitation' (this time with Edouard Balladur as prime minister), this decision was not challenged, as was reflected in the 1994 Defence White Paper. As a result, the army is to be severely limited in its ambitions for reform since overall numbers cannot be reduced below some 200,000 to 230,000 men (the threshold beyond which universal conscription would no longer be tenable) and there can be only a limited number of entirely professional units for force projection (in order to allow room for conscripts).

Funding

The second major impediment to the overhaul of French defence policy after 1989 – beyond politics – is funding. Confronted with

growing difficulties in the preparation of the new five-year procurement spending plan for 1992–6, the government decided to postpone
the whole exercise until the general election of March 1993. Consequently, for the first time in the history of the Fifth Republic, the 1992
and 1993 defence budgets were adopted outside the standard procurement plan procedure. For each of those two years, budgets of the same
amounts as the previous years were adopted, and this entailed a decrease
in real terms of some 2 to 3 per cent in 1992 and 1993. The procurement
section of these budgets decreased by 5 per cent each year (from 3.8 per
cent in 1988–9). Defence expenditure amounted to 3.2 per cent of
GDP in 1993, the lowest figure since 1945. One should also bear in
mind that the French defence budget includes appropriations for the
gendarmerie, whose functions are 90 per cent civilian. If this expenditure (9.3 per cent of the budget) is deducted, French defence expenditure for 1992 and 1993 is comparable with that of the Netherlands,
amounting to close to 2.8 per cent of GDP.

Without making drastic choices such as cancelling certain programmes altogether, the budgetary build-down was such that the
bottleneck in procurement would before long have caused collapse.
Unfortunately, no hard choices were made. Programmes were simply
extended (10 and 15 projects respectively in 1992 and 1993) and the
numbers to be procured were scaled down, all of which contributes to
further increasing unit costs of equipment to be acquired. Moreover,
the growing costs of peacekeeping or other operations conducted by the
French armed forces in 1992 and 1993 (2.5 billion francs for 1992 and
4.5 billion francs forecast for 1993) were systematically funded through
monies earmarked for procurement in each year's budget. The cumu-
lative result of this indecisiveness and inconsistency was in effect to
postpone any serious revamping of the ways and means of French
defence policy for several years.

Since the general election of March 1993, the budgetary issue has
not been resolved. In fact, the resulting *loi de programmation* voted in the
spring of 1994 is to be revised after two more years, half-way through
its implementation. It is broadly agreed that hard and fast choices will

be postponed until then, since by that time a new president of the republic will be in office and France should no longer find itself in the anomalous though recurring condition of 'cohabitation'.

The plight of the defence industry

The last and probably most significant impediment for French defence planners in adapting policy to the new strategic context has been the plight of France's defence industry. Much is at stake, economically and socially, in the future of the defence industrial infrastructure, badly hit since 1990 by cuts in the national defence budgets and loss of export markets. Generating annual sales of 150 billion francs (9 per cent of French industrial output), the defence industry employed 450,000 people in 1991, 200,000 directly. Of these sales, only 34 billion francs were generated by military exports in 1991 and 20 billion francs in 1992, significantly less than the 40 billion francs achieved annually during the 1980s. If this trend continues as forecast, the result could be the loss of 50,000 directly defence-related jobs and 80,000 indirect positions in the mid-1990s. The overall problem of production overcapacity in the French defence industrial base after the Cold War constitutes both a technical and a political problem which compounds difficulties in arbitrating between the plethora of procurement programmes. Conversely, any coherent policy aimed at the long overdue restructuring of the industry is impossible without the government signposting chosen sectors and technologies for future research, development and procurement. Yet dealing with the problem has been postponed twice, once until the 1993 general election, and then until after the 1995 presidential contest.

In sum, the essence of difficulties encountered by French defence policy in 1989–94 is encapsulated in the following contrasts. On the one hand, never since the 1960s have there been such powerful imperatives and pressures for thorough reform, but at the same time seldom have obstacles and inertia appeared as difficult to overcome. What is really at stake is the fate of a remarkably coherent defence model developed during the past 30 years, which is no longer appropriate to a radically altered strategic context.

The complexity and sheer financial as well as political cost of reforming this model are such that piecemeal measures are bound to prove inadequate. Nevertheless, for the reasons outlined above, the French government has, rightly or wrongly, confined itself to postponements and palliatives aimed at rationalizing the functioning of the system as a whole without reforming its structure. The stated goal of the many scattered measures affecting virtually all components of the armed forces – including the nuclear element – is to keep open as many options as possible while effectively preparing for the most radical ones in future years.

Reforms in 1993–4

It is scarcely surprising that successive French governments since 1989 have chosen to avoid a thorough overhaul of national defence policy. It is traditionally the task of the president of the republic to give the initial political impetus for any such overhaul. Yet the president's major pronouncements on the issue since the fall of the Berlin Wall have been few and far between. As indicated above, the closing years of Mitterrand's presidency (1993–5), involving 'cohabitation' with a conservative government, are hardly more conducive to decisive moves. Hence, the country's nuclear doctrine and defence strategy remain unchanged, at least in declaratory policy, while adaptation to the new international context has been attempted by means of numerous, minor measures, mainly under budgetary pressure. These measures were dramatically stepped up under Defence Minister Pierre Joxe (in office between early 1991 and the spring of 1993), gradually amounting to a defence review by stealth. As a result, it is not easy to present a coherent picture of what has been undertaken over the past two years, but the main trends can be summarized under three headings: first, an effort to trim down the French nuclear arsenal, without putting in question the primacy of strategic deterrence as an overarching concept in French defence policy;

second, a substantial effort aimed at improving the capacity to forecast and manage crises, especially by means of intelligence collection and analysis; and, third, an attempt to improve conventional force projection capabilities, notably by means of a reform of the French army structure.

Nuclear

In the nuclear realm, and for the first time since the beginning of military nuclear programmes in France, the 1991 and 1992 budgets have been decreased by 5 to 10 per cent on average. This has been a result of mothballing the Hadès substrategic surface-to-surface missile system (30 missiles are to be stored in eastern France), the withdrawal of all nuclear gravity bombs from the French air force, the decommissioning of one of the six strategic nuclear submarines, and the decision to replace the five remaining 'Redoutable' class by only four newer craft of the 'Triomphant' generation between 1995 and 2005. The new submarines will each carry 16 M5 submarine-launched ballistic missiles (SLBMs) equipped with six MIRVed warheads. Thus, around the turn of the century or soon thereafter, the French nuclear forces will probably evolve gradually into a strategic dyad of modern submarine-launched and air-launched systems. Indeed, the replacement of the current 18 Plateau d'Albion intermediate-range ballistic missiles (IRBMs) beyond the year 2000 appears unlikely. The issue has generated an intense debate since late 1993, and a number of prominent figures in the new parliamentary majority are in disagreement with President Mitterrand over that choice. No final decision, however, will be made before the 1995 presidential election, as stated by Defence Minister François Léotard in September 1993.

In the spring of 1991, the decision was taken to concentrate all airborne nuclear systems under the French strategic air command (FAS), thereby depriving the tactical air command of any nuclear role. As of autumn 1994, with the Hadès system mothballed, France nominally deploys only strategic nuclear forces (nuclear submarines and Mirage 2000-N aircraft equipped with the Air-Sol, Moyenne-Portée

(ASMP) stand-off missile). There has thus been a *de facto* adaptation of French nuclear deployment patterns to the new international setting, notably to cuts in the American and Russian arsenals. Tactical or prestrategic systems have been made redundant although the French air force retains the *functional* capability to deliver a prestrategic strike by means of the ASMP. This could provide France with a total nuclear arsenal of about 500 warheads by 2000/2005.

France's moratorium on nuclear testing since April 1992 was strongly criticized by the conservative opposition at the time. The moratorium was extended in November 1992 for another nine months, and once again in July 1993, after the advent of the conservative coalition to government. The latter decision was conveyed through a joint statement by President Mitterrand and RPR Prime Minister Balladur. The moratorium was maintained after the Chinese test of October 1993, in spite of dissent from the new parliamentary majority.

Intelligence

In the field of crisis management, intelligence collection and analysis, a substantial series of measures has been undertaken, both in budgetary and in organizational terms. This was indeed a favourite subject of Defence Minister Joxe, who made two important decisions. First, there was an overhaul and centralization of hitherto scattered defence intelligence organizations; and, second, the military uses of space were given top priority in research and development, and procurement. In the winter of 1991, the decision was taken to create within the Ministry of Defence a directorate for military intelligence to be placed under the direct authority of the Ministry of Defence and the General Staff. A directorate for strategic analysis was also created with the same intention of centralization. As for the military uses of space, net annual increases of 17 per cent were allocated on R&D for 1992 and 1993 with the overall goal of spending 85 billion francs on R&D and procurement between 1992 and 1997. This connotes a genuine political will to ensure for France a comprehensive though limited space capacity by the turn of the century by means of optical, thermal and radar satellites in orbit. All of these programmes have a European cooperation dimension, with a leading French role.

Restructuring the ground forces

The third major dimension of recent and current policy has concerned conventional power projection capabilities, whose necessity has been underlined so forcefully by the Gulf war and the complex logistical preparations it required. The key factor has been a restructuring plan for the ground forces. This plan comprised two main elements.

First, the command structure of the French army was discarded, as was its organization in two elements which dated back to the early 1980s (the Rapid Action Force for force projection, and the First Army). Under the new plan, to be fully carried out by 1997, the army's size is to be reduced from 280,000 to 225,000 personnel, from 12 divisions (of which five are armoured) in 1990 to nine divisions (including three armoured). These nine divisions, formerly part of the Rapid Action Force and the First Army, are to be reorganized as a single pool of forces out of which units can be drawn as required by three new national commands: a European command for allied operations in Europe, a force projection command for out-of-area operations, and a smaller special operation command for commando-type contingencies. The first two commands are to be fully staffed joint services commands.

The second major aspect of this reorganization is the drive towards European forces, notably by the assignment of one armoured division as well as the Franco-German Brigade to the newly created Eurocorps. Moreover, the political authorities will have at their disposal much more flexible options for out-of-area actions than in the past, notably for inter-allied operations as well as peacekeeping and peacemaking contingencies. But this remains somewhat theoretical, until the critical question of professionalization of the armed forces is settled. Indeed, even though the government has stressed the necessity for a higher proportion of professional soldiers, especially in units specializing in force projection, the decision to maintain a ten-month military service in the framework of a 225,000-strong land army will entail that the proportion of conscripts in 1997 will remain around 50 per cent overall (i.e., some 45 per cent of combat forces). Consequently, conscription will remain a major hindrance to force projection, even if the ground forces' structure has been quite thoroughly reformed since the Cold War.

Command reforms along the same lines have been implemented in both the navy and the air force, stressing in particular the necessity for airmobile force projection contingency planning. For the navy, the goal is to modernize the fleet while preserving the current levels of six nuclear attack submarines and 100 surface vessels, although the decision to procure a second Charles de Gaulle-class nuclear aircraft carrier to replace the Clemenceau-class ones has not yet been taken. As for the air force, 234 multi-role Rafale will be procured at a cost of 170 billion francs (R&D and procurement), with deliveries starting in 1996. The expense of the programme is such that the overall size of the fleet will drop to some 400 combat aircraft by the year 2000, thus falling below the current level of 450, consistently maintained since the late 1950s.

The 1994 White Paper

After a lengthy process of consultation and deliberation, France's new Defence White Paper was issued in February 1994. This was the first such exercise since 1972, and produced a very different sort of document. Whereas the 1972 edition was a statement of well-established strategic choices and orientations, the 1994 version reads like a preliminary framework for an as yet undefined future strategy. This is the result both of post-Cold War uncertainties and of the domestic political situation, which was hardly auspicious for decisiveness, let alone innovation.

Salient features of the White Paper include the acknowledgment that, for the first time in recent history, France no longer has any enemy in the vicinity of its borders. Also stressed is the growing importance of security issues such as weapons proliferation, terrorism, religious and nationalist extremism, and drugs trafficking, in a context characterized by the 'insufficiencies' of international order.

The responses outlined by the White Paper predictably include continued reliance on nuclear deterrence. But beyond a restatement of established policy, one may note a less orthodox reference to the need for a diversified and flexible nuclear arsenal, which some observers have interpreted as potentially opening the way to future nuclear strategies involving limited strike options.[3]

One of the most notable features of the White Paper is the greater emphasis on conventional than on nuclear forces and strategy. The enhancement of power projection is presented as a priority objective, aiming towards a personnel capability of 130,000. Yet, the White Paper reaffirms the case for national conscription on grounds of cost, involving the citizenry in France's defence, and the need to build up reserves and territorial defence.

In addition, the White Paper presents six scenarios of contingencies which may justify France's use of force. These are:

- a regional conflict not involving France's vital interests;
- a regional conflict involving vital interests;
- threats against France's overseas national territories;
- implementation of bilateral defence agreements, primarily with sub-Saharan African countries;
- interventions to uphold peace and international law, primarily in the framework of the UN;
- the resurgence of a major threat in Europe (considered the least likely scenario).

---

3. On this point, see the statements by Jacques Baumel, for example, of the National Assembly's defence commission, advocating deterrence from the 'weak to the mad' (*du faible au fou*) and the possibility of small-scale nuclear use against 'irrational' foes, as opposed to the traditional French version of deterrence from the 'weak to the strong' (*du faible au fort*) (*Le Monde*, 19 July 1992). Henri Conze and Jean Piq also argued in favour of developing more accurate and selective nuclear weapons. 'L'avenir de la dissuasion nucléaire', *Défense Nationale*, Feb. 1993, pp. 13–27.

More generally, France's forces are to be capable of taking part simultaneously in

- a major multilateral coalition operation (like the Gulf war);
- an intervention to protect a national overseas territory, or implementation of a bilateral defence agreement; and
- participation in an international peacekeeping operation.

Thus, the growing importance of multilateral operations and planning in French strategy is a characteristic feature of the White Paper, and indeed of recent French experience, whether in the Gulf, in Bosnia, or in Somalia. This also reflects the growing emphasis in France on the need for multilateralism, whether on a European, a NATO, or a UN level. In fact, with the exception of nuclear strategy and territorial defence, it is fair to say that France conceives of its own defence increasingly, if not primarily, in terms of coalition-building and concerted action.

3 GERMAN DEFENCE AND FORCE STRUCTURE PLANNING

Joachim Rohde and Hans Henning von Sandrart

German defence policy remains in a state of transition marked by severe financial constraints, with clear doubts existing about planned force structures. Defence capabilities and force structures reflect political interests and will, and a government's overall concept of its security and foreign policy. The German government has not yet clarified its thinking on the defence capabilities it wants or the price it will pay.

Defence planning

Any consideration of defence planning and its financial dimension must begin with the political factors of both internal and foreign policy which determine German security policy at the national and international level. The collapse of the Soviet hegemony and the resulting German unification raised questions in regard to defence which have been much more difficult for Germany to answer than for many of its European NATO allies, including the United Kingdom, France and Italy. To varying degrees these countries have been able to base their considerations on the continuum of national traditions, historical experience and strategic principles. During the Cold War the then Federal Republic of Germany had been well advised to show a low international profile in the field of security and defence policy and to pursue its interests only in the framework of the NATO alliance or West European multilateralism. The lack of any historical basis for defence policy scarcely mattered. Germany's pivotal role as a front-line state at the focus of the Soviet political and military threat, together with the quality and weight of the German conventional defence contribution, gave the German voice sufficient emphasis and influence in the processes of formulating the political interests of Western Europe and the alliance as a whole. Thus, for the German public national interests became identical with European interests and were obscured in a series of very general principles. The German forces and planning process were more closely integrated into and linked to the force structure and force goals of the alliance than were those of any other member state. For example, there was no proper military staff structure in Germany, either at service or at Federal armed forces level, for planning or developing a national military strategic or operational concept. Such matters were left to the alliance.

Since this low profile and voluntarily limited status served the Federal Republic well in the past, the German public has little awareness that the changed security environment and the new role of a united Germany at the centre of Europe require the formulation of German defence interests and the will and capacity to articulate them. This is necessary not only for Germany's sake but also because its European neighbours and alliance partners have an interest in how this new Germany is going to define its role and place in Europe and in the world. Such a debate is not yet properly under way in Germany, nor has any kind of broad consensus on the issue emerged. The debate must focus on the role of military forces as an instrument of a national policy which, in concert with allies and partners, guarantees national security and territorial integrity and fosters a political environment of peace and stability in Europe and beyond. As German armed forces were founded more or less solely in reaction to (and legitimized by) the overwhelming Soviet threat, it still seems difficult for Germans to understand the role of military force in the new security environment as a general instrument of state policy and with no specific target. Yet German defence and force structure planners must now make the necessary conceptual, structural, budgetary and investment decisions for the medium- and long-term future beyond the year 2000, despite the atmosphere of vagueness and indecisiveness.

The geostrategic fact is that Germany is located in the centre of Europe and many states bordering it regard this relatively strong country with a peculiar mixture of hope and fear. In addition,

Germany's welfare depends very much on exports, global freedom of trade and a stable European economic zone. Since future international security issues will be on a regional, if not a global level, Germany has a fundamental interest in international stability, conflict prevention and conflict management with the lowest possible level of forces. Like its major allies, it is convinced that future security risks and problems in an interdependent world should be managed and shaped in a multilateral framework. However, in contrast to England or France, Germany has no security or defence obligations outside its national borders other than those it has assumed through treaty. German citizens want to live in a world where state policy is directed through active international participation in structures such as the UN, the CSCE, NATO and the EU/WEU, and where this policy is guided by the norms of the UN Charter and the Charter of Paris.

National security interests

A number of vital German security interests may be identified:

* to protect Germany and its citizens against any kind of aggression and power-based political blackmail;
* to prevent, contain and, if at all possible, terminate through multinational action any crisis or conflict which could endanger the security of Germany or the European Union;
* to establish close cooperation and linkages with allied nuclear and maritime powers, since Germany as a non-nuclear and continental medium-sized power cannot shape the international order on its own;
* to make a substantial contribution towards strengthening and, if possible, enlarging the European integration process (EU/WEU), including the development of a European security and defence identity;
* further to develop and strengthen, as a partnership of equals, the transatlantic alliance, parallel to the realization of the European integration process, by supporting the continuation of the

American presence, both politically and militarily, in the security and defence structures of an integrated Europe;

- further to strengthen global and regional security structures such as the UN and the CSCE and to foster strong links with European defence structures including NATO and the WEU;
- to contribute to the continued development of democracy and a free market order worldwide, but especially in Europe, and with the main emphasis on the stabilization process in Central/Eastern Europe and in Russia;
- to improve stability, especially in and around Europe, by the active support of the arms control process and an effective policy promoting the non-proliferation of weapons of mass destruction and long-range delivery systems;
- to establish Germany as a source of economic and political stability, furthering European integration and cooperation in the heart of the continent, by consolidating the German unification process (which has proved to be much more costly and problematic than originally envisaged);
- to use Germany's economic, geostrategic and political weight in concert with its allies to strive for all these objectives and matters of national interest within the framework of international institutions and by multilateral policy-making.

Even this brief summary demonstrates that probably no other European nation has a greater interest than Germany in placing the pursuit of national interests within a multilateral framework of cooperation and integration. To put it the other way round, Germany would probably suffer most from a renationalization of defence and security policy in Europe. If military forces are to be properly used as instruments of state policy, it is obvious that defence and force structure planning, and the role assigned to the Federal armed forces by the government, should reflect a policy of stability, cooperation and integration based on national interest.

So far, the role of the Federal armed forces encompasses the following tasks:

- the protection of Germany and its citizens against political blackmail and any external threat;
- a contribution to the military-strategic balance in Europe and to the progress of integration there;
- the defence of Germany and its allies;
- the support of world peace and international security in accordance with the Charter of the United Nations;
- assistance in the event of natural disasters and emergencies and the support of humanitarian operations.

Leaving aside the constitutional/political debate in Germany concerning the legitimate range for international missions conducted by the Federal armed forces outside the NATO area, the set of missions approved by the constitution is broad enough to provide guidance for an adjustment of the force structure to the military requirements of a dramatically changed security environment and to redirect available resources (money and personnel) accordingly. The outcome of the troubling constitutional debate is therefore far less important for the actual defence and force structure planning than for the legitimacy of military missions in a wider international context, the acceptance of a wider range of missions by the public and by conscripts within the armed forces, and for the credibility of German security policy and of the role of the Federal armed forces as an instrument of integration and cooperation in the NATO alliance and Europe. But this is the political paradox the German defence policy has to live with until the constitutional debate comes to a conclusive end. Until then, the military forces will play their part in maintaining a strategic balance in Europe and contributing to stability through increased military cooperation. In particular, the military furthers integration both in the alliance and in the WEU by participating in multinational force structures. However, present political constitutional restrictions, combined with the limited capability to participate with allies and other partners in international peacekeeping and peace-enforcing operations, might create the impression that German forces are primarily oriented towards the task of national defence. This makes Germany for the moment an unreliable partner and thus diminishes German political influence in security-related matters.

Force structure planning

At present force structure planning in Germany is determined and, to some extent, constrained by a number of guidelines and factors.

The armed forces are be reduced to the internationally agreed personnel limit of 370,000 by the end of 1994, from a level of about 600,000 (which includes the East German armed forces [NVA – Nationale Volksarmee], added as a result of unification). This reduction has to be achieved in a smooth and socially acceptable manner which is also cost-effective. Such a drastic personnel cut in a comparatively short time cannot be achieved without drastic changes to the force structure, which necessarily creates disturbance. Also necessary is the absorption, disposal and/or conversion of large quantities of NVA equipment and ammunition in order to reach the CFE-agreed ceilings in the respective categories. Some elements in this process are costly.

The restructuring of the Federal armed forces as a consequence of German unification involves the achievement of a balanced garrison concept for the whole of Germany and the movement of some armed forces installations and training facilities into the new *Länder*. The garrisons and installations kept in service in eastern Germany have to be brought up to standard, environmentally and otherwise. This requires a considerable investment in infrastructure and social programmes now and in the future.

The enormous financial cost of German unification had been grossly underestimated, and the severe consequences for the Federal budget have been further aggravated by the economic recession. The shortfall has been met to a large extent out of those budgets which contain money for investment purposes such as the defence budget, which will probably reach its lowest level in 1994–5. This reduction exceeds by far the reduction which could reasonably be expected from the so-called 'peace dividend' after the end of the Cold War. Defence planners have found it hard to shape the successive cuts as a well-organized draw-down. As a result of this process, the investment part of the defence budget has dropped to roughly 20 per cent of the overall budget, making it impossible to maintain an orderly modernization process or to invest for new missions generated by the changed security environment. A ratio of 70 per cent to 30 per cent between running costs and investment costs is considered necessary to prepare adequately for the future.

Following the new NATO force structure categorization as laid down in the new strategic concept, the German armed forces will be divided into:

- The *crisis reaction forces*, comprising forces kept ready for any kind of crisis or conflict management or humanitarian operations within or outside Germany as part of multinational operations. Some elements will need to be ready for deployment at any time;
- *The main defence forces*, made up of all ready and reserve defence forces, including the reaction forces, and also those elements of the basic military organization which have a mission in the defence of national or NATO alliance territory. In the event of crisis or war the reserve part of the main defence forces will be brought up to strength and trained through a gradual mobilization system covering a period of up to 12 months. Such reserve elements could, according to their capabilities and the time available, be called up to reinforce the reaction forces;
- *The basic military organization*, comprising all elements which are required for running and managing the forces, for training, for mobilization and for supporting those alliance reaction forces which operate outside the central region. To manage these missions on a continuing basis the basic military organization will largely consist of existing forces.

Within this basic structure the armed forces will be organized and trained to take on new missions as part of multinational operations either in the familiar NATO or WEU framework or as part of ad hoc coalitions. The new character of the Federal armed forces has been described by the Defence Minister with the slogan 'ready to help and able to fight'.

More than that of any other NATO country, the German force structure will be heavily influenced by the concept of multinationality. German army elements will become part of multinational corps such as LANDJUT (covering the Jutland region), the Eurocorps, the GE/NL Corps, the US/GE Corps, the GE/US Corps and the Allied Rapid Reaction Corps. Despite additional financial burdens and some initial military deficiencies, the concept of multinationality is considered essential to keep the NATO alliance and the WEU together, and to work towards the required inter-operability which is the prerequisite for efficient military activity in the coalition.

Restructuring and adjustment

Changing the German force structure from what it was during the Cold War – totally dominated by the defence of the central region against a heavy armoured threat supported by a concentrated air threat – and adjusting the forces to a much more diversified mission range, including employment under quite different geographical and climatic conditions, will alter the profile of the services, which will in turn create new requirements for equipment and logistical and medical support.

The army has to find a new balance of heavy and light forces to meet the new requirements for tactical and operational mobility and flexibility which must in the end lead to an air mechanized capability. However, mechanized armoured forces will still provide the necessary strength on the ground against a modern well-equipped adversary. Therefore, as befits a continental state located in the centre of Europe, the army will remain the hard core of national defence and territorial integrity, even if, at present, no major threat on the ground is conceivable. For international reaction operations some other capabilities have to be expanded accordingly, such as those for transportable engineer, logistical and medical support and tactical air transport.

The air force will have to concentrate its efforts on air defence, both airborne and ground-based, including an anti-tactical ballistic missile (ATBM) capability, and on air transport. However, the air force must also retain a reasonable air attack capability with an accompanying reconnaissance and electronic warfare capacity. The air defence capability must ensure the integrity of the national airspace and provide for a limited out-of-area air defence capability as its contribution to multinational operations. The improvement of the air transport capability in both range and capacity should probably be pursued in a multilateral European framework.

The navy must improve its long-range, blue-water capability in order to participate in multinational sea operations. This requires a shift in emphasis from shallow-water to open-sea operations, with less emphasis on anti-submarine warfare capabilities. The anti-mine warfare capacity has to be maintained and enhanced for employment in more distant waters in order to meet possible threats to the supply lines of the industrialized democracies.

In order to focus limited resources on the highest priorities, the main financial effort will be devoted to the crisis reaction forces with the aim of providing a basic reaction capability by mid-1995, and a balanced and sustainable, if still limited, capability by 2000. All reaction forces should be ready for deployment by the end of the planning period. Establishing such a priority will necessarily lead to cuts and limitations in other fields, for instance in the reserves of the main defence forces, which are, at least for the medium-term planning future, considered less vital.

In addition to the restructuring and adjustment effort within the services, there is the need to improve some vital capabilities at the armed forces level, both for operational and military-strategic reasons and to economize. These changes include:

- establishing a national command and control capacity to allow the Defence Minister as the peacetime Commander-in-Chief to direct and control the German contribution to international operations worldwide, and to develop conceptual guidance as a basis for articulating the German position at the NATO alliance or any other multinational level of political control;
- improving the national intelligence-gathering and evaluation capacity required for out-of-area operations, and improving the

German contribution to an alliance and European strategic reconnaissance capability;

- improving strategic transport capacity to promote strategic flexibility and mobility. An air refuelling capability is needed. Such changes are achievable through alliance or, more probably, European cooperation;
- improving logistical and medical support not only for German reaction forces but also for alliance reaction forces operating from the central region;
- contributing to an adjusted alliance air command and control system (ACCS) and establishing a German share of an adjusted alliance/WEU integrated command and control structure capable of controlling crisis and conflict management operations.

The establishment and consolidation of such capabilities at the national armed forces level need to be closely linked, both conceptually and technologically, to alliance efforts or the multi- and bilateral efforts of the allies. NATO (or the WEU in concert with NATO) should have a clear responsibility, respected by all members, to harmonize these efforts to achieve the urgently required conceptual, operational and technical inter-operability that is urgently required. Inter-operability needs to be promoted effectively in multinational units in general if different national forces are to work together efficiently, and also to prevent the different multinational corps from going their own ways.

Budget constraints and expedients

The list of requirements contrasts sharply with the dramatically constrained budget situation as regards investment funds. Furthermore the procurement budget (in current prices) has seen a reduction of about 17 per cent between 1991 and 1992, 10 per cent between 1992 and 1993 and a further 18 per cent or so between 1993 and 1994. In real terms at constant 1987 prices, the decrease in the procurement budget from 1987 to 1995 amounts to between 65 and 70 per cent.

The best that military planners can hope for is the stabilization of the defence budget at the present low level. A relative improvement of the budget situation can only be expected when the economic and social burdens of unification have been fully funded. Although the proportion of German resources devoted to defence – expressed either as the percentage of GNP allocated to defence or as the defence expenditure per caput – never placed the country first in NATO rankings, in the past German real output produced the most formidable and modern conventional defence contribution in Europe. This was due to Germany's national conscription system, its cost-effective force structures, and the fact that it did not have to invest in a nuclear capability of its own. But at present and in the medium term, Germany must face budget constraints which are much more severe than those of most of its allies. This is probably the greatest challenge German force planners have had to face in the past 40 years. It will lead to a situation where the German armed forces, by international comparison, will fall back in terms of modern equipment, operational capabilities and diversity of mission capability unless decisive and serious planning decisions are taken to reverse this trend, at least for the vital reaction forces. The Ministry of Defence has embarked on a planning review in order to identify such measures and to obtain political approval. This may well be supported by a growing awareness among the public and within political circles of the severe consequences of this situation for the armed forces and thus for German security policy and the capability to cooperate internationally. Germany's capacity for integration into the NATO alliance and into European security structures on an equal and respected level is threatened.

Planning decisions which could correct this trend might consist of:

- further drastic rationalization measures in the field of operating costs involving training, maintenance, and logistical stocks not vital for the reaction forces and mobilization needs. Such measures will mainly hurt the parts of the main defence forces which are not vital for the reaction forces;
- the further curtailment of the procurement, modernization and equipment improvement programme;

- the further development of the garrison concept, if politically feasible;
- a balanced reduction in the personnel strength of the Federal armed forces, the creation of more cadre units, and a critical review of the defence strength after mobilization in order to achieve quality at the expense of quantity. For the moment the peacetime strength of the Federal armed forces is a sensitive political issue which may not be settled in the near future. A similarly sensitive issue is the future of the German conscription system. Although the military as well as most of the political leaders are convinced of the special value of the system, its future shape may be heavily influenced by several factors: the ultimate size of the German forces, the duration of national service, and the special requirements posed by reaction force capabilities in out-of-area operations;
- the positive review, in concert with allies, of possibilities for mission-sharing and role specialization at the NATO alliance or European level;
- the acceptance that participation in international operations will be funded from outside the normal defence budget;
- political approval for savings in the defence budget achieved by measures such as those mentioned above, mainly for the purpose of improving the investment budget, in order to return to an investment level of around 30 per cent as soon as possible.

The overall objective of defence and force structure planning has to be the stabilization of the planning process in order to complete the ongoing force restructuring in an orderly manner by 1995. This will then serve as the basis for shaping the armed forces for the future beyond 2000, and for maintaining German capability so that the country remains a respected, efficient and reliable partner for cooperation and integration.

Procurement and the defence industry

In the 1980s the equipment of the German armed forces, especially the German army, was comprehensively modernized. German companies consequently anticipated a moderate decline in the procurement budget for the 1990s and began to prepare for this by reducing operating costs (for instance by relocation), by concentrating capabilities and by diversifying into the commercial sector.

In the early 1990s this process was overtaken by events: as the costs of German unification were constantly revised upwards, the defence budget was reduced on an ad hoc basis from year to year. In these circumstances long-term planning within the Defence Ministry as well as within industry was (and from an industry standpoint still is) impossible. Each year industry was confronted with the cancellation of programmes and it was impossible to forecast which of the existing ones would survive. In early 1993 this 'adjustment' process culminated in the general halt to procurement ordered by Defence Minister Volker Rühe in order to gain time for a re-evaluation of all procurement programmes.

Meanwhile, industry had to develop its own estimates of the future medium- and long-term equipment requirements of the German armed forces and of the development of the defence (and especially the procurement) budget. During the adjustment process between 1990 and 1993 some 100,000 defence industry workers were laid off, and a further 40,000 are expected to follow by 1996. Within six years the German defence industrial base will shrink to half its 1990 employment strength. These lay-offs will cost the industry nearly 7 billion DM, which could otherwise have been available for research and development. This shrinkage was and still is almost devoid of political control. Nevertheless, at least some core capabilities will survive, and most of the larger German companies will probably still exist in 1995, although operating at greatly reduced strength.

For the German Defence Ministry the central question now is which capabilities to integrate and deliver complete weapon systems should and will survive this free fall, and how to ensure the maintenance of competitive manufacturing firms in Germany in the long term. There is a growing recognition, at least within the ministry, that Germany – to some degree against all its traditions – has to develop a defence industrial policy in order to reach this objective. As a first step, the Defence Ministry and industry have established working groups, whose objective is to advise the ministry on technological priorities, on the establishment of a dialogue with the defence industry about the nature and minimum size of capacities that are still economically viable, and on coordination/ synchronization with European allies on arms cooperation and work-sharing. These working groups have analysed not only the system level but also the component and subsystem levels and in some cases even the technology. There are five groups, dealing respectively with tanks and armoured vehicles; ammunition; aerospace (aircraft, helicopters, missiles); shipbuilding; and information technology/electronics.

It is now broadly accepted within industry and government that integrating European defence industrial capabilities is a prerequisite for maintaining German defence industries. The establishment of competence- and capability-centres in Europe is seen as a high priority, considering current diminishing defence autarky. However, this will require a different approach to arms cooperation.

Up to now arms cooperation projects have primarily been ad hoc and used as an instrument of national technological and industrial policy. They were established to maintain, to improve or to build up pertinent capabilities for defence on a broad scale. Consequently, national prerogatives with respect to arms procurement and also the actual manner in which arms cooperation was structured have led to over-capacity and then redundancies.

As a result, Germany is in favour of a new kind of arms cooperation, i.e., one that is no longer an obstacle to the rationalization of the European defence industrial base. Rationalization in this context means a process of industrial restructuring and specialization, which needs broad governmental support to begin and proceed. The detail should be left to defence companies in the light of their various capabilities to offer cost-effective equipment. Arranging this kind of work-sharing or specialization should be left to industry as far as possible without political intervention. This rationalization would require strategic cross-border dependencies and raises the question whether these would interfere with the national capability to use military power. So the question becomes: can this industrial rationalization take place outside the framework of a common European security and defence policy or do we have to wait until such a policy is implemented?

From a German point of view, work-sharing and specialization could and should take place even without a common security and defence policy within the framework of a European Union, because there are very few areas of military technology/capability in which national defence industrial capabilities are needed for military power to be exercised independently of other (European) states. This may be a typical German point of view because Germans find it difficult to envisage a situation in which their national forces would intervene except as part of a European/ transatlantic intervention force, i.e., one where industrial dependencies could bring political restrictions on the use of military power.

Conclusion

A trend towards the renationalization of defence planning may be discerned from several factors in European states: the development of special national capabilities; a stronger emphasis on formulating national interests and objectives; doubts about the future role of the alliance and the future of the European integration process; and perhaps the way in which defence budgets are being handled. In a superficial way such a trend may be real, but it requires a careful definition of 'renationalization'. If the model is the classical sovereign nation-state of the European past which jealously guarded its monopoly on power and considered itself the final product of history, then a trend to renationalization does not exist. All the European states which are partners in the European process and in the transatlantic partnership have already reached a position of close cooperation and integration. This has created a situation of mutual dependence which would be almost impossible to reverse without severe consequences. In addition, all these states have accepted and stated that the creation of a world order, or at least a European order of peace and stability, is possible only on the basis of multinational coordinated policy and action. What has developed at the end of the Cold War (and its unidirectional dominating threat) is a series of new, unpredictable and diversified present and future risks and threats to peace and stability which may have a different impact on the risk perceptions of allies and partners. In addition the focus of action may change among the various international security structures. In the past there was really only one multinational structure relevant for the North American and European democracies in defence and security matters, and that was NATO.

These changes require an assessment of the security consequences of a given crisis or conflict and a formulation of the national position before the multinational crisis and conflict management process can start and lead to multinational operation, either in the framework of the proven NATO alliance structure or of an ad hoc coalition. Such a national analytic capability seems to be a prerequisite for multinational action in the new and still fluid security environment. This will do no harm to NATO alliance or European solidarity or to the European integration process as long as it is kept under control with the clear objective of steering the national positions into the cooperative framework of multinational action. In addition, the alliance, or the WEU in concert with it, should be considered and respected as a key coordinator of conceptual harmonization and inter-operability. This is definitely the key interest of Germany as a medium-sized power in the heart of Europe. But German policy has yet to resolve the self-imposed paradoxical situation created by the constitutional debate, which for the moment could isolate Germany and make cooperation and integration hard to achieve.

The dramatic decline of the German defence industrial base, when industry is the main instrument for restructuring European arms cooperation (and thus for promoting European integration in the defence sector), has significant implications. Germany has never tried to become autarkic in this sector, and the economic importance of the defence industry for the rest of the economy is negligible. Therefore political pressure to 'buy German' is unlikely to develop on a large scale. The decline of the German defence industrial base is unlikely to lead to a renationalization of procurement policy but instead to a rapidly growing dependence of Germany on foreign sources and an accompanying inability to shape European and transatlantic relationships in this sector.

4 ITALIAN DEFENCE POLICY

Stefano Silvestri

Introduction

Italian defence policy has been deeply influenced by two factors: change in the international security situation after the disbandment of the Warsaw Pact, and the need to contain or reduce public expenditure.

The last official general review of the national defence policy was the 1985 White Paper (which was only the third since 1945). Each year since 1985, the Defence Minister has presented to parliament a *nota aggiuntiva* (supplementary report) to explain defence budget requests and to describe major policy and organizational issues. Then, in 1988, the House Defence Committee published the findings of its own investigation on major security changes, after which the Defence Minister, Virginio Rognoni, produced and presented to parliament in November 1991 the 'New Defence Model' (NDM). It was supposed to become the foundation for a new ten-year planning cycle, with important new investments and a reshaping of the armed forces. However, this NDM was not debated in parliament and has been variously revised, first by Defence Minister Salvatore Andò in 1993, and then by the armed forces themselves. A final edition of the revised NDM was published at the end of 1993. It aims at a major restructuring of the armed forces and at lowering expenditure, in line with the perspective of reducing the state budget in general.

The main problems around which these projects revolve are:

(1) the reform of the command structure;
(2) the transition from conscript to professional forces;
(3) the modernization of the military front-line and support

elements, coupling a further reduction of the field units with a ten-year funding increase in order to enhance the quality of major equipment;
(4) the costs of the entire exercise.

The first problem, although it has low political visibility, is considered crucial for streamlining important sectors such as operations, budget and procurement. Currently the Defence Chief is an essentially powerless broker, while the single service chiefs have effective authority over the fighting units and procurement. Slightly stronger is the position of the National Armaments Director (NAD), simply because over the years he has gained important *de facto* competences on all international programmes. Nevertheless the services still view his action as an encroachment on their exclusive prerogatives.

Before the last political elections in March 1994 the senate of the Italian parliament had passed a new law giving to the Defence Chief effective command over the entire military structure as well as the overall responsibility for planning. The General Secretary of the Defence Ministry (who is also the National Armaments Director) was to receive the military requirements from the Defence Chief, and to become the sole supervisor of all the administrative and procurement directorates of the ministry. The ministry would thus have had two functions, both directly linked to the Defence Minister. The other chiefs of the various military services, and all the general directors of the ministry, were to be subject to the authority of these two powerful figures. However, the Chamber of Deputies was unable to find the necessary time to pass this law, so, under the Italian constitution, this project will have to be submitted again to both houses by the new government.

The transition to more professionalized armed forces has been the subject of a highly visible and sometimes emotional debate. During the Cold War a conscript army – the army is personnel-intensive – was considered to be necessary not only from an operational point of view, but also to safeguard democratic institutions against possible *coups d'état* staged by a professional army. After the Cold War even the opposition dropped its hostility to professional soldiers and showed greater interest in a shorter conscription period and in the recruitment of professionals. From a strategic point of view the existence of fully professional units is widely recognized as the only means of strengthening collective security in the unstable post-Cold War environment. The exercise of the Gulf war drove home this point. However, the strongest opposition to professionalization still comes from the army itself, which does not see ways of funding competitive salaries for volunteers in times of financial crisis and which still wants to retain some 100,000 conscripts in order to staff a higher number of main defence and logistical units.

The government is attempting to promote the expansion of the number of voluntary soldiers: parliament has passed a law granting various advantages to volunteers signing up for three to six years in the forces and allowing for the eventual volunteer recruitment of women. The idea behind these proposals is to increase the number of volunteers from fewer than 20,000 to about 40–50,000 in the army alone, while reducing the number of draftees and of cadre or training brigades. Eventually, the number of professionals could increase still further.

The third problem has generated widespread consensus on the urgency of starting a major modernization effort to provide at least some units and components capable of long-range and 'out-of-area' operations. The last modernization drive was launched in 1975 with three special funding packages for each service and today there is awareness of key programmes in the areas of command and control, space, air and missile defence, strategic transportation and electronic warfare which depend on the availability of additional funding and timely procurement decisions.

The fourth issue is the most delicate. Currently the defence budget fluctuates around 26,000 billion lire (at the April 1994 rate of exchange, slightly more than US$16 billion), only 70 per cent of which is apportioned to the Defence Ministry proper (the rest being spent on the Carabinieri (21 per cent), pensions (8 per cent), and other expenditures (1 per cent). The NDM required major spending increases in the form both of defence budget rises and of a special equipment programme law. The total additional expenditure, over ten years, was estimated in

1991 at about $50–56 billion. There is open conflict between the austerity programme implemented by the most recent governments and these financial objectives. Thus, expectations of spending associated with the NDM have been cut back, perhaps to a total of about $15 billion over the next ten years (mainly for investment) on top of present budget allocations.

The Defence Ministry is attempting to confront these problems in a unified way, and is asking parliament to grant some 'delegated powers' to the government through a *legge delega* – a 'framework law' which would establish principles and aims and empower the government to issue a pre-specified number of decrees regulating the detail. The debate is moving away from the revised version of the NDM and will be settled, hopefully in 1994, by the new government. In principle, two out of the three political parties making up the winning coalition have called for an increased defence budget. The third (the Northern League) is also asking for greater investment expenditures and for the creation of an 'all-voluntary army core', while aiming at the same time to maintain the draft, to be organized under regional militia-like formations.

Thus, the situation is currently in a state of flux. We have to consider three different realities: the armed forces as they are now, the prospects introduced by the NDM, and the changes that may be decided by the new parliamentary majority and the new government.

Foreign policy and strategic thinking

Italian defence policy recognizes the changes in the strategic scene. While the main threat of the Cold War years has vanished, 'small wars' multiply and new direct and indirect risks emerge out of a general situation of uncertainties, economic underdevelopment and social turmoil. Thus, as of now, the UN and other international institutions are the main political reference points of Italian security policy. Italy concurs with the main emphasis of the policy advocated by the UN Secretary-General, to increase the effectiveness of UN mechanisms and means. The Italian government has reacted positively to the Secretary-

General's 'Agenda for Peace', but has not yet decided to support its specific recommendations.

A second reference point is the CSCE. The Italian belief is that the CSCE should be stronger institutionally, have clearer legal bases and promote stabilization policies (especially through crisis prevention). The main idea is that, while the UN and the CSCE are the major depositaries of international legitimacy, they should utilize or encourage other international organizations (such as NATO or the WEU) to play a greater security role under their supervision. Italy feels that NATO and the WEU have taken a similar stance. That of NATO in particular – an adaptation process, characterized by greater openness and cooperation with Eastern countries, including the CIS republics – is considered very useful and positive by the Italian government.

The WEU's emerging dialogue with the East is also favoured by the Italian government. As far as the relationship between these two institutions is concerned, Italy continues to support the proposals made by the Anglo-Italian document of October 1991, believing that there is no contradiction between building the WEU as the military dimension of European Union and maintaining NATO, where the WEU will play the role of the European pillar. The important thing is to develop effective international operational means for crisis management.

A large popular consensus sanctions Italian membership of NATO. This organization is seen as an indispensable collective mechanism to guarantee national security and as an effective force multiplier. While Italy favours the Partnership for Peace initiative, it also considers that the European Union should extend its membership to include the Central/East European countries. This would raise the problem of the eventual enlargement of NATO to take in the new members of the EU, or alternatively of a large reappraisal of NATO's functions and role.

Some voices raise the question of non-proliferation (and the future of the Non-Proliferation Treaty), of new threats from weapons of mass destruction and of the future of nuclear deterrence asymmetries in Europe. The predominant opinion is that, to avoid greater risks of renationalization of defence, NATO should try to confront these questions and find a way to manage them.

As far as the WEU is concerned, the Italian government believes that three tasks should be confronted:

• the creation of a new European defence identity, i.e. the WEU, as an integral part and military arm of the European Union;
• the reorientation of the various national defence models towards a greater convergence and operational integration; and
• the compatibility between the new European defence identity and NATO.

The Italian armed forces should perform three main 'missions'. The first is a function of 'presence and vigilance', involving a variety of civilian and military means, and is mainly national, even if it includes participation in related functions accomplished by NATO and eventually the WEU. The second mission refers to the defence of 'external national interests' and to contributions to national defence. NATO (or WEU) commitments are included in this function, as well as crisis management missions. The third function is the 'integrated defence of the national space': while less urgent, this is also the most intensive mission and could require the full mobilization of national assets. Finally, the armed forces should stand ready to assist in the defence of the democratic institutions and to help the population in cases of grave natural catastrophes.

Italy is ready to contribute, as far as possible, to international peacekeeping or peacemaking missions, provided that they receive some kind of UN or CSCE legitimization, and/or that they are carried out in the framework of NATO, the WEU or the Western system at large. It is also ready to assume some strictly bilateral commitments (such as the guarantee of Maltese neutrality, or the provision of humanitarian aid to Albania), provided that these do not conflict with larger political engagements and indeed can be seen as the logical extension of such engagements.

Two main obstacles may hamper the implementation of such missions: the fact that most of the Italian armed forces personnel are conscripts, and the technical limitations of the operational forces.

Technical shortcomings include a lack of sophisticated intelligence gathering systems (satellites), advanced mobile command and control means, up-to-date early warning capabilities, strategic mobility and 'intelligent' weapons. Yet the main problem is the lack of experienced officers and specialized training. This obstacle is particularly relevant for the army, where the experience of participation in UN missions both in Somalia and Mozambique has demonstrated that conscripts can be employed, if at the expense of a greater turnover of personnel and some reshuffling of units. The navy has normally employed its conscripts on operational vessels on out-of-area missions, but only where they constitute on average less than 25 per cent of the crew. The air force has employed professional personnel only on out-of-area missions.

In the past, external military commitments have gathered adequate domestic political support and have been relatively popular, but no major loss of life has been experienced. The reaction to the killing of Italian servicemen in former Yugoslavia and (more to the point) in Somalia has not involved the popular rejection of these commitments. In all these cases, however, it is professional or volunteer soldiers who have been killed. The main reaction seems to be that these commitments should be pursued, but that greater guarantees should be sought, both in the political field and in terms of self-defence capabilities. In general, public opinion seems to favour commitments that promise clear and relatively rapid solutions.

While the Italian constitution 'repudiates war as a means to solve international controversies', this has never been read as precluding Italian participation in military operations, provided that they are legally or morally justified. Still, the government has only narrow powers to mobilize Italian assets and use military forces without explicit parliamentary backing. Formally, the constitution states that 'the Parliament decides the state of war and gives to the Government the necessary powers'. Thus, short of a formal state of war, it seems that the Italian government has some freedom of initiative, provided that it does not need nor ask for exceptional powers. Parliament is normally 'consulted' by the government before any resort to military force, but no formal vote has been requested. Problems have arisen,

however, when an intervention could not be funded through existing
budgetary allocations and parliament has had to be asked for money.
The government has suggested solving this question either by a
constitutional change, or more simply by a new law regulating the
relationship between parliament and government during military
crises other than outright war. No formal proposal has yet been
submitted to parliament.

The defence budget

Defence expenditure

The 1993 defence budget amounts to 26,110 billion lire, apparently a
real increase of about 5 per cent over the 1992 budget of 24,517 billion
lire. However, the 1992 budget had been originally set at 26,017 billion
lire, and then abruptly cut, for national financial reasons, at mid-year.
Thus, in reality, the 1993 defence budget is almost identical to the one
originally set for 1992.

As noted, the defence budget includes some expenditure related
only indirectly to defence. In particular, the sum of 7,377 billion lire is
allocated to the Carabinieri (the Italian military police force which
includes about 115,000 men and is employed mainly in domestic and
judiciary police roles) and to advances on retirement payments. Other
minor expenditure is related to missions of civilian assistance. Only
18,633 billion lire ($14.44 billion) is for defence proper. The most
recent version of the NDM plans a steady but significant increase in
defence appropriations, to reach the level of 21,500 billion lire ($16.7
billion) in ten years. In practice, the real defence budget oscillates
around 1.5 per cent of GDP, the lowest percentage among the major
European countries.

The main structural problem of the Italian defence budget is the high
percentage of personnel expenditure within the total budget. This falls
if only defence appropriations are considered. (The personnel expenditure of the Carabinieri accounts for about 80 per cent of its total
allocation in the defence budget.) Nevertheless the share of defence

spending on personnel is higher than that of countries such as Germany or Great Britain, and Italy spends comparatively little on investment and the acquisition of new weapon systems.

However, the defence budget is not necessarily an accurate guide to actual expenditure, and Italy's defence industry has had some protection against cuts. The Italian defence budget includes a high level of *residui passivi*, sums allocated to a heading but not actually spent within that category during the year in question.

What is more worrying in the short term is that the budget for operational expenditure (including training) is already extremely low and decreasing, which explains some structural Italian problems when demanding military missions are considered.

Figure 1 shows the growth of the Italian defence budget between 1985 and 1993 (at constant 1985 prices). It is interesting to observe that the appropriations for the defence function reached their peak in 1989, and that their decline was about to be reversed in 1993. (The 1994 budget has been maintained at the level of 1993). However, expenditure on the Carabinieri has experienced continuous growth, thus demonstrating the relative weakness of the defence establishment in Italy, and the low priority given to defence proper, especially when compared with domestic security, anti-terrorism and police operations. When the normal police forces (though not those led by army generals[1]) are included, as well as the border guards and the other armed services of the state (such as the Forest Guard or the Warder Guard), the total number of Carabinieri, professional and armed servicemen exceeds 280,000 men – greater than the present strength of the Italian army (220,000).

Figure 2 shows a ten-year projection of the defence budget according to the most recent version of the NDM and the total amount of investments projected (61,000 billion lire over ten years).

---

1. The defence budget allocates expenditure only to the Carabinieri, which also has specific allocations in the budgets of other ministries (interior and justice). The other armed services are fully funded by other ministries.

Figure 1: Defence budgets (at 1985 prices)

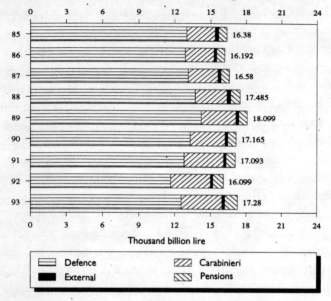

Figure 2: Projected defence and defence investment spending

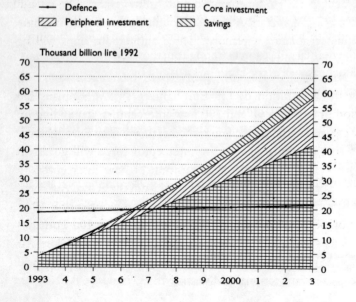

Manpower and force structure

Table 1 outlines the planning in manpower terms. In organizational terms, the army, which had 26 brigades plus 3 mobilization brigades in 1990, now has 19 plus 3. The planning in NDM 91 was for 15 plus 4 brigades but, according to the most recent version of the NDM, the target now is for 12 or 13 brigades, with no mobilization units. The army will be reduced from its present 70 battalions to 45–50 battalions. It is not yet clear what kind of units will remain. NDM 91 (with 15 operational brigades) envisaged the existence of 8 mechanized brigades, 2 armoured brigades, 3 Alpine brigades and one paratroop brigade. The 12 or 13 brigades of NDM 92 will probably see a cut in mechanized brigades. It is possible that one will be transformed into a new amphibious brigade (together with the existing marine battalion of the Italian navy), or that an independent amphibious regiment of 2 battalions will be formed.

The navy will be based on one main operational group which could be divided into two operational sub-groups involving a total of 18 major surface combatants (instead of 20 in NDM 91) and 8 submarines (instead of 10). It will have two cruisers, of which one is already a through-deck cruiser to be equipped with short/vertical take-off and landing (V/STOL) aircraft. A second through-deck cruiser with some amphibious capabilities is planned. Three amphibious ships will be operational as well as three fleet support ships.

The air force has presently 146 F-104S interceptors and was planning the acquisition of 130 Eurofighters. NDM 92 plans the acquisition of between 90 and 106 new interceptors, depending on the price tag (and without specifying whether they will be Eurofighters). In terms of operational groups the interceptor force will go down from 8 to 4 or 5. Pending the acquisition of new interceptors, a number of Tornado ADVs are being leased from the Royal Air Force and some modernization is being carried out on a number of F-104s.

The bomber force will remain untouched, based on 100 Tornados organized in 4 groups (3 of bombers and 1 SEAD). The Close Air Support (CAS) force, presently based on 310 aircraft in 11 groups, will be reduced to 175 operational AMXs and MB-339s plus 36 RF104-Gs,

Table 1: Manpower and force structure, 1991–2

	1992	NDM 91	NDM 92
Total officers	35,650	29,280	29,000
Total NCOs	89,192	76,500	68–70,000
Volunteers-cadets	21,221	57,800	67–81,000
Conscripts	214,166	123,000	50–86,000
Total forces	360,229	287,080	230–250,000
Army	233,722	177,500	135–150,000
Navy	49,488	43,580	39–40,000
Air force	77,099	66,000	56–60,000
Civilians	56,131	45,000	40–44,000

	Configuration of the forces			Differences	
	% in 1992 (present)	% in NDM 91	% in NDM 92	NDM 91 over 1992 (%)	NDM 92 over 1992 (%)
Officers	9.9	10.2	11.6/12.6	−18	−19
NCOs	24.8	26.7	28/29.6	−14	−22/24
Volunteers-cadets	5.9	20.1	26.8/35.2	+172	+216/282
Conscripts	59.5	42.9	21.7/34.4	−43	−60/77
Army	64.9	61.8	57/60	−24	−36/44
Navy	13.7	15.2	16/17	−12	−19/21
Air force	21.4	23	24/26	−14	−22/27

organized in 7 groups (some other AMXs will remain in reserve status).
The transport groups currently number 3 with 12 C-130s and 41 G-
222s. This number will rise to 4 with the acquisition of 12 more long-
range transport aircraft.

Main programmes

The main acquisition programmes divided by service and according to
the 1993 budget are:

Army: CATRIN battlefield communication and information
   system
Infantry weapons cal. 5.56 mm
Folgore anti-tank rocket
Ariete main battle-tanks (MBT) (heavily reduced)
Centauro heavy armoured car
Light armoured cars
Mangusta A-129 light attack helicopter (status uncertain)
MLRS heavy multiple rocket launcher (heavily reduced)
FIROS-30 heavy multiple rocket launcher
Skyguard/Aspide low altitude surface-to-air missile (SAM)
Do-228 twin turboprop light transport aircraft
Night vision goggles (NVG) systems
Nuclear, biological, chemical defences

Navy: EH-101 Anglo-Italian anti-submarine warfare (ASW)
   medium helicopter
Sauro conventional attack submarine
AV-8B Plus (V/STOL aircraft)
Second Garibaldi Class V/STOL cruiser (not yet
   commissioned)
S. Giorgio class LPD to be used also as training ship
MU-90 Italo-French light torpedo
MILAS stand-off naval ASW torpedo launcher missile
Sonar Italo-French for the future S-90 submarines
New generation naval surface to surface missile (SSM)
Electric engine for the future S-90 submarines

Air Force: AMX Italo-Brazilian light attack plane
Eurofighter (UK-Germany-Italy-Spain)
F-104 enhancement programme
Unspecified smart weapons (most probably laser-guided
   GM and anti-radiation missiles)

National Armaments Director:

    FSAF Italo-French naval point defence missile

    HELIOS (France-Italy-Spain) IR photographic satellite

    NH-90 (France-Germany-Netherlands-Italy) medium
        ASW/tactical transport helicopter

    SICRAL secure telecommunications satellite

    CTPs (Common Technological Projects) sponsored by
        Western European Armaments Group (WEAG)

    EUCLID WEAG initiative

    MIDS Nunn Amendment programme

    ADSIA Nunn Amendment programme

Also of interest is the list of the programmes which had featured in earlier official statements but have now been tacitly dropped. While they continue to have some nominal prospects, they may never again win defence appropriations.

Discontinued programmes:

    SIACCON, one C2 army battlefield management system

    VCC-80 AIFV, some 800

    10-ship new generation frigate class

    Patriot SAM, 20-9 batteries

    Tornado ECR, 16 aircraft

    Airborne Warning and Control System (AWACS),
        2 aircraft

This simple listing of programmes reflects the dominance of bureaucratic inertia in a defence ministry committed to across-the-board modernization and the maintenance of commitments made during the Cold War. There is no apparent contemporary strategy to select priorities and to guide choices. Private interviews confirm such inertia. This programme will certainly be reviewed according to the NDM 92, but the work is still under way. The main impetus for a drastic reduction in the number of programmes, unless political choices are made at a higher level, is the severe general financial situation which, of course, also affects the defence budget.

5 DUTCH DEFENCE POLICY

M. van den Doel

Introduction

The end of the Cold War gave the Dutch government the impetus critically to examine existing defence policy. This involved a discussion of conscription as against an all-volunteer force, as well as analysis of the armed forces and their operational functioning.

The 1991 Defence White Paper made projections regarding the size of the military forces at the end of this century following a thorough reorganization and a reduction in personnel. The reorganization of the Dutch military forces, begun in mid-1991, is expected to take eight years and should lead to a smaller but more flexible organization prepared for the challenges of the twenty-first century. The CFE Treaty offered the opportunity to reduce forces, especially the army, as did the withdrawal of the troops of the former Soviet Union from Eastern Europe.

An update of the Defence White Paper was issued in January 1993. The collapse of the Soviet Union and the rapid changes in the security situation necessitated more radical changes than those first projected. The planned reduction of military forces by the end of this century will now lead to approximately 40,000 fewer military personnel than the 128,000 in 1991. (This number refers to the standing forces in peacetime, not the wartime organization with mobilized reserves of about 100,000.) The restructuring of the armed forces, especially the army, and the suspension of conscription (as of 1998) are the most radical changes in Dutch defence policy since the Second World War.

With the end of the East–West conflict, the chance of small-scale wars has increased, thereby boosting the importance of crisis management. This requires the modification of military forces, with the greatest consequences for the army.

The changed security situation requires an appropriate political attitude. The Netherlands is prepared to meet its international responsibilities, which means that military forces can be used for operations both within and outside the NATO area. The new security situation requires increased flexibility and mobility. As part of NATO plans, the Netherlands contributes to the Allied Rapid Reaction Corps and main defence forces. The country is thus ready to provide land, air and sea forces for use either in crisis management or in a large-scale conflict, as necessary. Operations outside the NATO area would preferably take place under the auspices of the United Nations. The government will examine each political situation to determine whether a military contribution is necessary and, if so, in what form. For operations within NATO, the operational concept 'mobile counter-concentration' applies. It is difficult to apply a general concept for operations outside the NATO area, as the location, the nature of the problem, and the extent of the operation are not known in advance. However, flexibility and tactical and strategic mobility are clearly desirable. The restructured armed forces must be prepared not only for the classic role of defending the NATO area, but also for new tasks such as humanitarian aid, conflict prevention, peacekeeping and peacemaking.

This chapter gives a brief outline of Dutch security policy in general and then covers in more detail defence policy as it relates to the role of the parliament, conscription, the defence planning process, the restructuring of the Dutch armed forces, the defence industry and *matériel* policy, and international cooperation.

Dutch security policy

The altered security situation in Europe has consequences for the different security institutions. The UN, NATO, the WEU and the CSCE are all concerned with preventing and controlling conflicts. The Netherlands is in favour of an effective division of tasks among these organizations.

The Dutch preference is for political and military cooperation within the framework of NATO, which is considered to be the organization best suited to maintain stability on the European continent. As an organization for collective defence, NATO has an integrated military structure, and the necessary means and expertise to carry out its tasks. Now that the US is planning to withdraw many of its troops from Europe, the European NATO members will have to bear a greater responsibility for the defence of the continent. Although the enhancement of the role of the WEU is logical, this should not happen at the expense of NATO. The Dutch government sees the WEU as a bridge between the EU and NATO, assisting in the unification of Europe and strengthening the European pillar in NATO. The decisions taken at the NATO summit in January 1994 were a major step forward. The Combined Joint Task Forces Concept (CJTF) enables Europe to undertake its own responsibilities within the framework of NATO. This has consequences for the contributions of the European countries. The Gulf war showed shortcomings in the area of air-lift and sea-lift capability. During the Cold War, had the General Defence Plan been implemented, 'wagon-pooling' would have been used to transport tanks and caterpillar-tracked vehicles. Similarly, NATO and the WEU today need to pool capacity for sea and air transport. The Netherlands is prepared to offer military units for use in the WEU, not exclusively, but to be shared with NATO and hence answerable to both organizations. The operational role of the WEU is complementary to that of NATO. There will be no Dutch contribution to the Eurocorps, although Dutch participation in joint exercises of the WEU and Eurocorps is possible. With this approach, the Netherlands continues to follow the political line of recent decades, in which NATO formed the cornerstone of Dutch security policy.

Nuclear weapons and ballistic missiles

Now that the nuclear roles of the Lance missile, artillery and anti-submarine Orion aircraft have been dropped, the Netherlands has only one nuclear task in the alliance: its F.16s are capable of executing nuclear missions. However, the London Declaration has designated nuclear weapons as 'truly weapons of last resort', and the Dutch stress that since nuclear proliferation must be reduced and limited, NATO should be the only organization with nuclear means. A separate nuclear role for other European organizations such as the WEU and Eurocorps is rejected.

To reduce the dangers of ballistic missiles, the Missile Technology Control Regime (MTCR) should be strengthened. The Netherlands supports the initiatives in a NATO framework for the study of a Global Protection System against ballistic missiles.

The role of parliament

The involvement of the Dutch parliament in defence matters has increased significantly in recent years. At the beginning of the 1960s, the government appointed the members of the Defence Commission, which met in closed sessions. Now all political parties are represented and the meetings are, in principle, open to the public. Only the Commission for Intelligence Services is made up of a limited group, coming from the largest groupings in the parliament. In the past, the Defence Commission has met far more frequently for consultations with the Minister of Defence. The greater involvement of the parliament can be explained by an increased integration of society and the military over the years, the development of labour unions for military personnel, and, of course, the changed security situation.

Parliament has the responsibility of overseeing the budget, which means that all defence expenditure must be approved by it. The annual budget presentation is not limited to financial elements, but also covers all the relevant policy aspects, thus providing a good overall picture of the defence position. The budget is handled in a plenary session of the parliament, which discusses all aspects of security and defence policy. Long-term policy is presented in the government's Defence White Paper.

The close involvement of the parliament with defence is also reflected in the many visits of parliamentarians to military installations and the written questions submitted by them concerning defence policy. When far-reaching changes are proposed, the Defence Commission can hold hearings to help form more enlightened decisions.

The increased influence of the parliament on defence policy can be seen, for example, in two motions which have been passed to the effect that conscripts can only be sent to places outside the NATO area on a voluntary basis, and that Dutch participation in operations outside that area must meet strict criteria, according to which participation is only possible in an international framework, preferably on the basis of a resolution by the UN Security Council; and in the event of 'peacekeeping' outside the UN framework, all involved parties must be in agreement with one another.

It is also possible to intervene 'out of area' for emergency humanitarian operations to stop or avert massive violations of human rights. Yet the Yugoslav conflict has shown us the change in the peacekeeping landscape. It is sometimes hard to make a clear difference between peacekeeping and peacemaking efforts.

Conscription policy

The Netherlands has a mixed-cadre conscript armed force. The army is dependent on conscripts for 60 per cent of its personnel. Only about 38 per cent of conscripts approved for service actually serve, which creates unequal burden-sharing and has reduced support in Dutch society for maintaining conscription. Opinion polls have indicated that the majority of the Dutch population opposes conscription, and changes in the security situation have brought about even more debate on the issue. In 1992 a study by a commission appointed by the Minister of Defence reported, in 'Towards New-style Conscription', that conscription should not be abolished, but that the period of service should be shortened to nine months and changed in form to make it more attractive. Transition to an all-volunteer force would be expensive and the study indicates that it would be difficult to find sufficient available candidates on the labour market. In addition, the constitution would have to be amended. According to the commission, the Dutch political–military effort should not be dependent on the labour market.

However, public and parliamentary political support for maintaining conscription was lacking and a parliamentary decision was taken in June 1993: in a wholly professional military organization the active personnel in the armed forces will drop to 70,000 by 1998. The conscription system will be suspended – not abolished – to enable conscripts to be called up again should the international security situation deteriorate. With effect from 1 January 1994 the period of conscription is reduced to nine months. As from 1 January 1998, there will no longer be conscripts in the Dutch armed forces. However, doubts still remain and objections have been raised by army analysts. The availability of sufficient numbers of volunteers in the Dutch labour market has continued to be questioned. Concern has also been expressed regarding such a large reduction in the size of the army. Compared with the conscript army, a decline in personnel quality is also expected. It is feared that military service will prove unpopular and lead in the long run to a smaller and less credible army.

The defence planning process

The Dutch defence organization is composed of a 'line-staff' structure, in which the military branches are directly responsible to the Minister of Defence. The ministry functions as a 'holding company' with the military branches as 'subsidiaries'. Since 1974, the so-called Integral Defence Planning Process (IDPP) has been used to make policy, with planning based on instructions and guidelines from the ministry. This is a cyclical process which begins and ends in the Defence Council. The planning process takes place on two levels: that of the military branches and that of the ministry. Coordination between and within the levels is assured by different task-oriented committees in which all military branches are represented, and by departmental consultation. This process determines tasks and resources. The coordination and fine-tuning of plans within a branch of the military is the responsibility of the commander. The Chief of the Defence Staff is responsible for coordination between the different branches.

The 'Defence Equipment Selection Process' is a part of the total planning procedure and guides large investments and equipment spending. Based on this procedure, projects are set up with arrangements for interim checks and for any alterations necessary on the basis of the wider defence planning. This Defence Equipment Selection Process ties in with the Periodic Armaments Planning System (PAPS) which is used in NATO and in the former Independent European Programme Group, now the WEU Armaments Group.

Planning and financing

Good planning requires knowledge of long-term available financial means, and financing should be independent of short-term economic developments. Analysis of the security situation and the tasks necessary, with their means of performance, form the primary input for the defence budget. Until 1990, when the 1978 'three per cent' agreement within NATO was used as the basis for planning, there was real annual growth. On the basis of the altered security situation, there has been a substantial reduction since 1990, involving a slower pace of investment. From 1994, a zero-growth defence budget is currently planned, but after the parliamentary elections in 1994 a new coalition government will have to determine the guidelines for the defence budget. For a long time, the division of the budget among the military branches was determined by a set formula. Although this system has not been formally used since 1989, not much has changed in practice. Approximately 50 per cent of the budget goes to the army, with the navy and air force each receiving about 25 per cent. Tables 1–3 provide details of defence expenditure and budgets.

The Dutch armed forces

The main tasks of the Dutch armed forces are:

- to contribute to crisis management operations, including the delivery of rapid deployment units for use in an international framework outside the NATO area (UN, CSCE);

Table 1: Planned Dutch defence expenditure, 1992–6 (guilders, billion)

Year	Amount	Year	Amount
1992	14.2	1995	13.6
1993	14.1	1996	13.6
1994	13.7		

Table 2: Changes in real development defence budgets, 1990–94 (%)

Year	Annual change	Cumulative change since 1989
1990	–4.1%	–4.1%
1991	–2.6%	–6.6%
1992	–2.7%	–9.1%
1993	–6.5%	–15.0%
1994	–2.3%	–17.0%

Table 3: Composition of the defence budget (%)

	1990	1992	1994
Operating expenditure	76.2	77.0	70.7
Personnel	53.9	52.4	50.7
Equipment	22.3	24.6	20.0
Investment	23.8	23.0	29.3
Equipment	18.6	17.9	22.2
Infrastructure	5.2	5.1	7.1

- to contribute adequately to allied (NATO) defence;
- to protect the territory, airspace, and territorial waters of the Kingdom (the Netherlands, the Netherlands Antilles and Aruba).

In order to perform these tasks, military organization and means must satisfy the requirements of flexibility, mobility, inter-operability, and multifunctionality. Tables 4 and 5 give a breakdown of the personnel in the Dutch armed forces, and the apportionment of the defence budget.

The Royal Navy

The Dutch navy operates to prevent the outbreak of war and to manage crises in times of tension, by a maritime presence and by participating in allied exercises. Naval units are part of multinational forces such as the Standing Naval Force Atlantic, Standing Naval Force Channel, and Standing Naval Force Mediterranean. Naval forces are, by nature, mobile and flexible, both strategically and tactically. This means that the altered security situation has few major consequences for the organization, structure, and resources of the Dutch navy.

Naval forces were not dealt with in the CFE Treaty and the maritime balance of power has barely changed. Thanks to the altered security situation, the prospects in the maritime sphere are better than they were before 1991, when the Soviet Union still existed as an entity. This justifies a lower operational availability and, ultimately, the disposal of a number of ships.

The Dutch navy functions in task forces which operate independently or in conjunction with others. A maritime task force consists of a frigate for command and control, an air defence frigate, six other frigates (the surface combatant fleet), a supply ship, ten helicopters, six maritime patrol planes (Orion) and two submarines. The navy can form three task forces, one of which will be put on reserve in 1995 and will then be disbanded around the year 2000.

Table 4: Dutch armed forces personnel: professionals and conscripts, 1990–97

	1990	1993	1997
Royal Navy			
Professional military	15,439	13,410	12,426
Conscripts	1,563	1,563	1,563
Royal Army			
Professional military	23,895	21,447	21,345
Conscripts	41,122	31,121	25,226
Royal Air Force			
Professional military	13,144	11,994	9,953
Conscripts	4,195	2,820	2,216
Royal Military Police			
Professional military	3,546	3,430	3,386
Conscripts	400	512	265
Central Organization			
Professional military	638	600	551
Conscripts	200	174	155
Defence (total)	126,191	106,970	95,899
Professional military	56,662	50,881	47,661
Conscripts	47,480	36,190	29,425
Civilian personnel	22,049	19,899	18,813

Table 5: Budget allocation to branches of armed forces, 1990–94 (guilders, billion)

	1990	1992	1994
Royal Navy	2.7	2.9	2.7
Royal Army	5.8	5.4	5.0
Royal Air Force	2.7	2.6	2.6
Royal Military Police	0.3	0.3	0.3
Central organization	1.2	1.4	1.3
Payments to former employees	1.4	1.6	1.6
Civil defence	0	0	0
Multi-service projects	0	0	0.2

Force Structure 2000 (Active):

Frigates:	16	Helicopters:	20
Supply ships:	2	Minesweepers:	17
Submarines:	4	Marine battalions:	3
Patrol planes:	13	Amphibious transport ship:	1

The Royal Army

In the coming years, army manpower will be reduced by 54 per cent. This reduction is possible because of the CFE and CFE-1 agreements and the radical changes in the security situation. These factors have resulted in a thorough reorganization of the army. To meet the new requirements of mobility and flexibility, a mobile air brigade will be set up. Operational in 1994, the brigade will have access to transport helicopters (30) and attack helicopters (40). The mobile air brigade will be part of the NATO Rapid Reaction Corps. In this way, the Netherlands can contribute substantially to crisis management. Due to the changes in East–West relations, the total number of active units will be reduced. From 1998 on, when conscription will have been abolished, the entire army will consist of volunteers who can carry out all crisis management tasks.

Some features of the restructured army are:

* there will be a combined army corps with Germany as of 1995, consisting of one Dutch division and two German divisons. The corps headquarters will be located in Münster (Germany);
* brigades will be made more suitable for more flexible and mobile action in a multinational framework;
* the emphasis will be placed on a small but adequate active force with fewer reserve units. There will be just two reserve brigades in 1998 and one more may go;
* one logistically independent division will be formed;
* there will be a shift from heavily equipped to more lightly equipped, more mobile units;
* there will be a more favourable relationship between combat and combat support units (teeth-to-tail ratio).

Force Structure 2000 (Active):

One division made up of:

- 1 mechanized brigade
- 1 light brigade
- support units
- 1 air mobile brigade (not in the structure of the division).

In reserve will be two mechanized brigades (the need for which will be evaluated in 1998).

The Royal Air Force

The tasks of the air force in peacetime and time of crisis consist of air policing, air defence (from the ground and in the air), combat support for land and sea forces, air reconnaissance, and air transport. The CFE Treaty has no consequences for the size of the Dutch air force. However, because of the improved overall security situation, its active level can be reduced. One means of achieving this is to reduce the number of operational combat planes and to place in reserve Patriot ground-to-air missiles. Like the navy, the air force maintains all necessary mobility and flexibility, and major organizational changes on the basis of the altered security situation are not necessary. To improve the tactical and strategic air transport capacity, transport planes currently in use will be replaced. The strategic air transport fleet is also suited to the air-to-air refuelling role.

Force Structure 2000:

Combat planes, F-16:	122
Air transport (fixed-wing):	
Strategic capacity:	2
Tactical capacity:	6
Observation helicopters:	29
Transport helicopters:	30
Attack helicopters:	40

Air defence:
4 firing units Patriot (20 launch units)
8 firing units HAWK

Defence industry policy

The Dutch defence industry is small (1.25 per cent of total industry), but high in quality. Research and development are also limited. A large part of the defence industry consists of component supply companies, while the Dutch defence organization buys most of its major systems from foreign suppliers. The Ministry of Defence does not automatically buy parts and consumables from Dutch manufacturers, although Dutch industry is kept informed of new needs. It is the task of the Dutch Ministry of Economic Affairs to create the conditions for good entrepreneurial performance in the country as a whole. The Dutch Defence Ministry is reluctant to incur increased costs by buying from local firms rather than foreign industry.

From the national military-strategic viewpoint, there is no need for a major Dutch defence industry. In times of crisis and war, the basic requirements for the logistical support of operations can still be met largely by industrial facilities and factories, assuming that conflicts would be resolved quickly. In peacetime, the navy relies on its own maintenance assets. In crisis and war, it needs extra support from civilian factories and shipyards. In general during the Cold War period, there was no need for local industrial facilities making products with a long production time, and the solution was the procurement of adequate additional stocks of high-consumption items. Whether or not this policy needs to be revised, owing to the changed security situation, has not yet been decided. In general, policy-makers are convinced that the present situation is preferable.

In a larger European and transatlantic context, the Netherlands has the capacity to make a high-quality technological contribution. However, as the national need is insufficient for a viable Dutch defence industry, the Defence Ministry gives only limited support to the promotion of exports, within the constraints of the Dutch weapon export policy.

When it is necessary to buy new equipment, the products on the market are checked for availability, quality, standardization and inter-operability, and logistical cooperation with the allies is explored. If there is no suitable product on the market, attempts are made to set up a cooperative development project with allies.

Equipment plans

Navy

In the coming years, a number of frigates and two supply ships will be replaced (one in 1994 and the other in 2000). An amphibious transport ship will be deployed, possibly in 1996. The 20 helicopters in use will be replaced by the NH-90 in about 2000. The Netherlands will build coastal minesweepers in cooperation with Belgium and Portugal. Six Dutch minesweepers will be replaced at the end of the decade.

Army

Almost all the equipment plans for the army are geared to the improvement of mobility. The largest investment concerns the acquisition of attack and transport helicopters for the air mobile brigade. Improvement of the reconnaissance, security and surveillance capacity is also desirable. The armoured tracked vehicles for reconnaissance will be replaced by light armoured wheeled vehicles. The reconnaissance capacity will be broadened by the acquisition of a Remotely Piloted Vehicle (RPV) system.

Air force

An expansion of tactical and strategic air transport capacity is planned through the acquisition of two KC-10s and approximately nine smaller transport planes.

International cooperation

NATO

Active naval forces are almost entirely at the disposal of NATO. There is permanent participation in three Standing Naval Forces and the maritime patrol aircraft operate under NATO control from the Keflavik base in Iceland. The Netherlands provides three marine battalions (including support) for use in the ACE (Allied Command Europe) Mobile Force which, jointly with the British navy, is part of the UK–NL Amphibious Landing Force.

The army contributes an air mobile brigade to the NATO Rapid Reaction Corps and one division in the German–Dutch army corps to NATO main defence forces. A so-called light mechanized brigade is stationed in Germany as part of the 'forward presence'.

The air force has made 144 F-16 fighter planes available to NATO in peacetime. From 1996 onwards this number will be reduced to 108.

The United Nations

The Netherlands has always contributed to UN operations according to circumstances and ability. With the role of the UN increasing as a result of the changing security situation, sufficient support from member states is more vital than ever. The Dutch government is very aware of the importance of UN operations and has therefore contributed, in 1992 alone, to the peace operations in Cambodia (UNTAC), Angola (UNAVEM), Croatia (UNPROFOR-I), and Bosnia and Herzegovina (UNPROFOR-II). Dutch UN observers are active in the Middle East (UNTSO) and until 1994 in Sinai in the non-UN multilateral force.

The Netherlands has no units specially trained for UN work and in principle all kinds of units are available for UN tasks. If units are assigned, the personnel receive special additional training. There is as yet no permanent assignment of units to the UN, but the Netherlands is ready to contribute 2,000 men to a stand-by UN force.

Equipment

The Netherlands works together with many countries on military equipment. The new minesweepers were developed in cooperation with Belgium and Portugal, and a new supply ship with Spain. The Netherlands also participates with Germany, France and Italy on the NH-90 helicopter project. The navy does maintenance work on certain weapons systems for Belgium, and Dutch facilities maintain the Harpoon missiles of Denmark, Germany and Greece. The air force works together with Germany and the US in the Patriot Post-Deployment Build Programme. The army cooperates with Germany on standardization and improvement of the Leopard tank. Other international cooperative programmes, some involving training, are listed in the Appendix to this chapter.

Matériel policy

The Netherlands gives high priority to international cooperation on *matériel*, with preference for cooperation within Western Europe. Cooperation helps to reduce overcapacity and to encourage political cohesion between like-minded countries. Through cooperation on *matériel*, standardization and inter-operability increase and costs decrease, while the competitive standing of the West European defence industry improves.

The Dutch government would prefer to bring West European defence *matériel* cooperation into the sphere of the European Union. The Netherlands would like to drop Article 223 from the EEC Treaty, or to change it so that a distinction is no longer made between civil and defence industry. The European Union is in a better position than other bodies, organizationally and legally, to see that new regulations concerning the defence *matériel* market are observed.

APPENDIX: ADDITIONAL INTERNATIONAL COOPERATION

The United States: The American Air National Guard provides training programmes for the Dutch air force.

Canada: The Dutch air force uses training facilities for practising low-altitude flying at Goose Bay.

Germany: The Dutch army is working with Germany to set up a bi-national army corps as part of the NATO main defence forces. A Dutch brigade is permanently stationed in Germany.

Belgium: There is cooperation with Belgium on *matériel* and training of naval personnel including a Belgian-Dutch minesweeping school. A bilateral agreement is due to be signed, though this is in doubt as a result of a Belgian review of defence policy.

Great Britain: Cooperation in the naval sphere consists of joint exercises of the UK-NL Amphibious Landing Force.

Central Europe: On a ministerial level, there are bilateral agreements with Hungary, the Czech Republic, Slovakia, Poland and Romania. An agreement with Bulgaria is in preparation. It is principally concerned with advice and assistance in the restructuring of the armed forces, common exercises, the clean-up of severely polluted military exercise terrain, support in establishing an air defence system and advice on the coordination of civil-military air traffic.

6 BRITISH DEFENCE POLICY

Trevor Taylor

British defence policy since the end of the Cold War has been marked
by both continuity and change. Important judgments and elements of
force structure from the post-1945 period remain in place, although
significant reductions in spending and manpower have been made.
Moreover, there is little sense that the process of adaptation to the end
of the Cold War has been completed, even by the latest round of
changes announced in July 1994 in the *Front Line First* report.[1]
Uncertainty about the future is unavoidable, given that British defence
policy has not developed either a clearly resource-led or a capability-
led foundation. In other words, Britain has not decided on a force
structure for whose maintenance it will pay whatever is necessary, nor
on an amount which it is ready to devote to defence over the long term.

That the British government has been unable to specify either the
resource or the capability fundamentals of British defence policy reflects
in turn a lack of consensus about the country's overall role in the
management of security on the global scale. Britain maintains forces in
part to contribute to the maintenance of international peace and
stability, but just what sort of contribution should be made, and of what
size, has not been defined by the government. As Christopher Bellamy
has pointed out, Britain has the expertise to serve as a 'global
mercenary', a 'soldier of fortune' leading the West European military
intervention capability.[2] However, fear of casualties, of long-term

1. Ministry of Defence, *Front Line First: The Defence Costs Study*, London, HMSO, 1994.
2. See C. Bellamy, 'Soldier of fortune: defining Britain's new military role', *International
Affairs*, vol. 68, no. 3, July 1992, pp. 443–56. This was one of the three articles in the
same issue (the others being by Christopher Coker and William Wallace) on 'Britain's
place in the world'. See also William Wallace, 'Foreign policy and national identity in
the United Kingdom', *International Affairs*, vol. 67, no. 1, Jan. 1991, pp. 65–81.

commitments and of high economic costs has prevented the emergence of such a role so far.

The fundamental element in the adaptation of UK defence policy after the Cold War was the secret governmental 'Options for Change' exercise which led to the announcement of a broad new force structure in July 1990,[3] well before NATO agreed its own envisaged force structure in the spring of 1991 and its New Strategic Concept in Rome in November 1991. Publicly, however, the UK stressed that Options for Change was a provisional exercise which could be adapted after consultation with allies. Before looking at changes in force structure and specific policy, this chapter discusses four factors which have had, and are continuing to have, a marked impact on defence policy.

Influences on defence policy

The US dimension

The first factor is the British historical experience with the United States. When the British contemplate the twentieth century, they note that, at times when the US has been militarily present in Western Europe, it has first proved a decisive influence in major wars and subsequently been associated with extended peace on the continent. Given British cultural links with North America and the close cooperation which was established in war and afterwards between the defence and security organizations of the two countries, it is not surprising that Britain feels Europe is more secure with a US presence. Britain has obviously had difficult experiences with the US, most obviously over Britain's interest in becoming a nuclear power after 1945 and over the Suez crisis, but on the whole British governments would not see themselves as having paid a heavy price for their intimate relationship with Washington.

British leaders tend to assert that Europe cannot be secure without an American presence, but they rarely explain why. During the Cold War it could be said that only the US could balance the USSR, but that

3. Statement by Tom King, Secretary of State for Defence, to House of Commons, 25 July 1990, *Hansard*, vol. 177, no. 150, Col. 470.

argument is rapidly losing relevance except with reference to Russian nuclear forces. It is difficult to perceive among British political elites any fundamental belief that, without the US, West Europeans would inevitably quarrel among themselves and the European Union would break up.[4] There appears instead to be a deeply rooted, simple inclination to see Europe as safer with the United States than without it, and certainly the British have tended to see the US as a less problematic leader of Western Europe than any state on the continent would be.

During the Cold War, Britain worked to establish and keep the US commitment. In particular it accommodated American forces and nuclear weapons, demonstrating that the UK was carrying an appropriate share of the defence burden. It developed a rationale for its own nuclear forces, carefully presented as both independent and assigned to NATO, which argued that they reinforced the US nuclear guarantee for Europe. On matters beyond the NATO area, Britain was often more sympathetic to US choices than were some continental NATO allies. Finally Britain promoted West European solidarity so that the US could see it was working with a coherent group of allies who took their defence seriously. The British role in the formation and development of the Western European Union and the Eurogroup must be seen in these terms. However, Britain was and is reluctant ever to push West European defence cooperation to the point where the US might feel that it was neither wanted nor needed in Europe.

Nevertheless, the end of the Cold War made a US withdrawal more conceivable, whatever Britain did. There was by the early 1990s a debate in official circles in which some participants (particularly from the Foreign and Commonwealth Office) argued privately that NATO could not survive as a significant organization without a threat from Russia. Consequently West European cooperation came to be seen as more significant (in general, Defence Ministry officials are much more reluctant to accept such a conclusion). Since 1990, British security policies have been based on the logic that it would be preferable for the

---

4. As Josef Joffe appears to believe, and even Manfred Wörner did.

US to stay but, if it left, West Europeans should remain in alliance, and defence in the area should not be renationalized. There has also been slowly growing acceptance that the US might prefer a coherent West European partner rather than a fragmented group of states. Hence the genuine UK commitment to the strengthening of the Western European Union.

Taking defence seriously

A second background factor is that defence since the Second World War has been taken very seriously by British governments. The lesson of the 1930s was that neglect of defence can lead to disaster, as it almost did in 1940. During the Cold War, Britain tended to spend rather more of its national product on defence than its major European allies, and its armed forces were broadly provided with the particular equipment they needed rather than something which it was thought would sell well in foreign markets.

Significantly, the historical experience of the British is that when they have taken appropriate defence preparations seriously, they have been largely successful in their use of force. Luck has played its part in this but there is in Britain widespread confidence that the armed forces will succeed in operations where they themselves anticipate success. The decisive factor leading to the British action against Argentinian forces in 1982 was the positive reply which Mrs Thatcher received when she asked military leaders if they could retake the Falklands. Nine years later, there were few doubts among the British public that the UK air forces and enhanced brigade in the Gulf would complete the tasks to which they had committed themselves.

Curiously for a country which has so many demonstrations of military ceremony and pageant, the British government sees the prime purpose of its armed forces as the deterrence of possible enemies and the defeat of aggressors. The UK has opted for professional forces because they are thought to be the most cost-effective soldiers and politically useable in a range of situations. There is no equivalent to the continental belief that the task of the armed forces is to strengthen, through conscription, the emotional commitment of the population to an ideal of serving the nation. The Ministry of Defence has been reluctant to see itself as having responsibilities for UK employment or wider technological advance: it sees its job as the preparation and operation of Britain's armed forces. This rather unromantic attitude towards defence has specific consequences: in particular, in the 1980s and 1990s it made the British especially interested in procurement techniques which could generate optimum value for money in terms of defence capability.[5] It may be that this refusal to burden armed forces with politico-atmospheric roles beyond strictly military tasks has also made Britain reluctant to exaggerate the capabilities of its forces for reasons of political convenience. Thus, in the post-Gulf war period, Britain insisted that Western Europe could not avoid reliance on American help for significant military interventions beyond the NATO area (while France preferred to stress the autonomy which Europe in the long term could achieve). Clearly the end of the Cold War has eased the pressures on the need to defend Europe directly and has opened up the possibility that more resources could be devoted to wider interests, should the need be there.

The UK's global outlook

Third, Britain was until comparatively recently a major imperial power and has traditionally derived much of its wealth from trade. It still has specific if dwindling responsibilities (for the Falklands, Hong Kong and Gibraltar); it has kept close security ties with some states for which it was formerly responsible (especially with the emirates of the Gulf and with Southeast Asia, where Britain is a member of the Five-Power Defence Arrangement); and it retains a keen interest in international relations worldwide. For a country of its size and wealth, Britain maintains a large number of well-staffed embassies and a significant intelligence effort.

5. See T. Taylor and K. Hayward, *The British Defence Industrial Base*, London, Brasseys, 1989, Ch. 5.

Until 1990 Britain was forced by economic circumstances and the growth in Warsaw Pact strength to devote more and more of its military resources to Europe. In 1968 the crucial decision was taken not to deploy forces east of Suez after 1971. But formal defence policy and the structure of forces maintained left Britain with a real sense of concern for the wider world, which its permanent seat on the UN Security Council helped to sustain. The Defence White Paper of 1985 argued:

> Exports account for some 30% of Britain's gross domestic product. We therefore have a strong interest in seeing peace and stability maintained in the countries constituting our trading partners; in securing the supplies of oil and strategic materials that are vital to our and other Western economies; and in keeping open key trade routes. The prosperity and security of the Western world rest on a complex framework of relationships, not just between the developed, free economies but also with others in less prosperous and stable regions. While no Western country, and certainly not the United Kingdom, can carry alone the burden of sustaining this framework, neither can any Western country dissociate itself from a share of the responsibility for doing so.[6]

While these words, written when the Soviet military capability was still increasing, reflect to a degree a debate in the West on burden-sharing which was under way at the time, they point to a British tradition of wanting an intervention capability in the wider world. However, this feeling for military intervention must be reconciled with the various reasons for and against such activities, which raise some problems.

The indivisibility of peace

There is no British consensus as to whether international peace should be seen as indivisible. Among British political elites there is no clear

---

6. *Statement on the Defence Estimates 1985*, Vol. 1, para. 217, Cmnd 9430-1, London, HMSO, 1985.

commitment to the belief that aggression anywhere, if unchecked, will lead to further aggression, either by the original wrongdoer or by others who feel they can imitate it with impunity. Historically, on the one hand, the failure to check Germany, Italy and Japan in the 1930s has given Britain some reason to believe that aggression anywhere is a cause for major concern, and in the Falklands and Kuwait crises it was common to hear British leaders assert that aggressors must be punished. On the other hand, Britain is reluctant to envisage potential involvement in every conflict anywhere. The British government knows it does not have the resources to be a world actor. Even where it feels it has major immediate interests at stake – and the Gulf is the most significant such region outside Europe – it recognizes that in future it could act militarily only in concert with others. Its preference would be for Western Europe to be sufficiently capable and willing that it could act as a valuable partner of the United States and on occasions be ready to act with only limited American help. European self-sufficiency is not abjured as undesirable in principle but in practical terms is seen as being beyond the resources which will be made available.

The British government is not alone in having no confident answers to the issues outlined here. Where it is clear, however, is in seeing the military instrument as an appropriate and occasionally necessary method of rectifying an aggression, especially when that aggression has been recognized as such by the United Nations, when no less costly means of remedy are available, and when military intervention itself can be expected to be successful at an acceptable cost to Britain. It welcomes situations such as that in Western Europe where the threat and use of force plays no part in international politics, and it sees the use of force as justified only by defensive causes, but it offers no endorsement of pacifist principles.

A related issue concerns the United Nations. A terse version of British attitudes would say that the UK, with its permanent place on the Security Council, is happy to see the UN playing a prominent role in the international order, especially since use of the veto has in practice ceased and the General Assembly is no longer dominated by non-aligned causes. However, Britain would not want to rely completely on a Security Council enabling resolution before British military intervention could occur: China and Russia are not yet viewed as completely reliable partners in issues of international order. During the Kuwait crisis Britain argued that an explicit resolution permitting 'all necessary means' (Res. 678) was not necessary to justify military action by the coalition, since the Council had already defined Iraq's action as aggression.

The present British government recognizes that its armed forces have and will have roles other than deterrence and periodic combat; indeed, a significant proportion have been engaged in policing Northern Ireland since 1969. Historically, Britain has also provided peacekeeping forces abroad, especially for the UN operations in Cyprus. Its recent experience would suggest that it will contemplate even costly and risky military action against an aggressor if that action, once begun, can be completed quickly. Developments in Kurdistan and Bosnia suggest that it will also provide forces for what seem likely to be longterm peacekeeping duties, although the greater the perceived danger to UK forces, the greater is British reluctance to be involved. Britain, like other WEU members, accepts that traditional defence, peacekeeping and humanitarian relief roles will all be played by national armed forces.

In summary, the 1992 Defence White Paper explained that UK 'defence policy would best be defined in terms of three overlapping roles:

- To ensure the protection and security of the United Kingdom and our dependent territories, even when there is no major external threat.
- To insure against any major external threat to the United Kingdom and our allies.
- To contribute to promoting the United Kingdom's wider security interests through the maintenance of international peace and stability.'[7]

The three roles were not seen as being in any order of priority. The vague and open-ended nature of the third role mentioned is readily apparent.

7. Essay on 'The United Kingdom's defence strategy' in *Statement on the Defence Estimates 1992*, Vol. 1, Cmnd 1981, London, HMSO, 1992, p. 9.

Spending levels and patterns

Britain traditionally has spent more on defence than its major European allies. Table 1 digests information from the 1992 and 1994 UK Defence White Papers which shows, for instance, that by 1991 Britain was spending much more than Germany on defence (using all three indicators), despite being a poorer, smaller country. After 1991 the dollar value of the UK defence effort was reduced by the fall in value of sterling.

Britain's stated intention is to have smaller but better forces, i.e. fewer personnel and units which are, however, better equipped and trained. According to the original Options for Change exercise, between 1990 and 1995 British forces were to be cut numerically by 20.1 per cent, less than the average cuts planned across NATO, and defence spending was scheduled to fall by a much smaller percentage.

However, the financial situation was difficult to see clearly, partly because of the special costs which were being incurred during the first half of the 1990s. These covered redundancy and other payments to service personnel losing their jobs, the charges associated with reorganizing and relocating forces, and the costs of replacing stocks lost during 'Operation Granby' (the UK contribution to the liberation of Kuwait).[8] Also blurring the picture were the removal from the defence budget of pension payments to retired service personnel, and the transfer of security and intelligence expenditures from the MoD to the Cabinet Office. Table 2 gives basic data.

Each autumn the British government announces its spending plans for each ministry. According to the 1991 Statement and the 1992 Defence White Paper, 'we anticipate a reduction in the defence budget of some 5.5% in real terms between 1990–91 and 1994–5 (excluding the costs of the Gulf and redundancy provision) ... Over the same period, defence expenditure as a proportion of GDP, excluding Gulf costs, is expected to

8. According to the government, the direct costs associated with the Gulf deployment in 1991–2 were £803 million, while £1,525 million was received from other governments as a contribution to the total costs of the war.

Table 1: Indicators of defence effort: 1991 and 1993

	Defence expenditure as % of GDP		Total defence expenditure (US$m)		Per capita defence expenditure (US$)	
	1991	1993	1991	1993	1991	1993
United Kingdom	4.2	3.7	42,716	35,257	742	608
France	3.5	3.4	42,399	42,593	748	738
Germany	2.6	2.0	39,893	38,629	499	481
Italy	2.1	2.1	23,583	21,185	409	365
Netherlands	2.6	2.3	7,242	7,039	482	461

Source: Statement on the Defence Estimates 1992; Statement on the Defence Estimates 1994.

Table 2: Future UK defence spending

Financial year	Cash spending plan (£m)	Financial year	Cash spending plan (£m)
1993–4	23,450	1995–6	22,130
1994–5	22,890	1996–7	22,230

Source: Statement on the Defence Estimates 1994.

fall from 3.9% to 3.5%.'[9] However, throughout the early 1990s the MoD came under constant pressure from other parts of government, especially the Treasury, to cut its spending, and the reductions made somewhat exceeded those envisaged. By the summer of 1994, British real defence spending in 1994–5 seemed likely to be about 8 per cent less than it had been in 1990–91.[10] Further significant cuts were scheduled for 1995–6

9. *SDE* 1992, op. cit., paras 302 and 303. These figures do not obviously square with the 1991 autumn estimates, which show that, in constant 1990–91 pounds sterling, defence spending should fall from £21.8 billion in 1990–91 (net of other governments' contributions to the Gulf conflict) to £20.8 billion in 1994–5, a drop of only 4.5%: 1991 estimates published in the *Independent*, 7 Nov. 1991.
10. A calculation based on Table 1.2 in Government Statistical Service, *UK Defence Statistics*, London, HMSO, 1994. The 8 per cent estimate discounts the effect of the removal of service pensions (more than £1.6 million) from the defence budget.

and 1996–7: for 1994–5 planned spending was £21.3 billion (in 1992–3 prices) and that for 1996–7 was £20 billion, a fall over two years of 6.1 per cent.[11] By 1996–7, defence spending was expected to be 2.9 per cent of GDP. There was the additional possibility that planned spending might be further reduced, most obviously in the expenditure plans to be announced in the autumn of 1994. In July 1994 the House of Commons Defence Committee observed critically: 'No plan seems to survive the next public expenditure round. Every activity is reviewed and revised again and again.'[12]

How is money being spent? Table 3 illustrates some trends since the mid-1980s, showing changes in the cash value of equipment spending and the shares taken each year by general support research, development and production, and development, production and repair for land, air and sea systems. The air systems category includes helicopters used by all three services and the Harrier fixed-wing aircraft used by the Royal Navy. Comparable data for the period after 1992–3 are not available, because the government has amended its definitions of research and development, resulting in the reclassification of some expenditures. There are several striking aspects of the data.

Most salient is the fall in procurement spending, particularly notable in 1992–3. This fall reflected budgetary restrictions and increased personnel costs associated with redundancy payments and force restructuring. Land, air and sea systems were all affected, although air equipment spending could be seen as the most protected. As of the summer of 1994, the government had published no plans for equipment spending proper (i.e. with 'associated costs' of over £1.1 billion a year arising from the procurement process being deducted) to attain the sort of share of the overall budget (over 45 per cent) which it had reached in the mid-1980s. However, equipment's share could rise above its currently envisaged maximum (38 per cent) as a result of savings from the 'Front Line First' exercise being kept within the defence budget and

11. See *UK Defence Statistics 1994*, op. cit., and public expenditure plans reported in the *Independent*, 1 Dec. 1994.
12. Quoted in 'Leave defence spending alone, report urges UK MoD', *Jane's Defence Weekly*, 9 July 1994.

Table 3: Trends in equipment procurement expenditure (£ million at current prices)

Expenditure	1985–6	1988–9	1989–90	1990–91	1991–2	1992–3
Total equipment	8,978	8,902	9,527	9,863	10,842	9,872
Equipment procurement share of total defence exp. (%)	50	46.7	45.9	44.2	44.1	41.5
General support exp. on equipment	1,297	1,629	1,785	1,784	1,969	1,982
of which exp. on general research	399	386	448	411	466	545
Sea systems	2,499	2,633	2,890	2,955	3,142	2,891
Land systems	1,887	1,554	1,738	1,927	2,157	1,846
Air systems	3,296	3,085	3,114	3,197	3,574	3,152

Source: Government Statistical Service, *UK Defence Statistics*, London, HMSO, 1994, Table 1.4.

used for equipment. The findings of the exercise, and the job cuts associated with them, were announced simultaneously with major MoD contracts and invitations to tender worth £5 billion.[13]

As Table 4 shows, throughout the changing political circumstances since 1985, the respective shares of land, sea and air systems in the procurement budget varied comparatively little, reflecting a UK commitment to balanced forces, inter-service bargaining outcomes,

13. 'Equipment orders survive surgery', *Financial Times*, 15 July 1994; 'UK weapon buys offset budget blow', *Defense News*, 18–24 July 1994; 'MoD sweetens cuts with equipment buys', *Jane's Defence Weekly*, 23 July 1994. Immediate contracts were announced for seven Sandown minehunters (£250 million), 259 Challenger 2 tanks (£1.1 billion), the upgrade of 142 Tornado GR1 aircraft (£700 million), 400,000 rounds of 51 mm mortar ammunition (£50 million), and Paveway 3 laser-guided bombs and their laser designators (L300 million). Interest was expressed in the purchase of US submarine-launched Tomahawk missiles and of a conventionally armed air-to-ground missile. Tenders will be sought for replacements for Britain's two assault-landing ships, and submarine and frigate orders were also envisaged.

Table 4: Changing shares of the equipment procurement budget (%)

	1985–6	1988–9	1989–90	1990–1	1991–2	1992–3
General support equipment spending	14.4	18.3	18.7	18.1	18.2	20.7
of which research	4.4	4.3	4.7	4.2	4.3	5.5
Sea systems	27.8	29.6	30.3	30.0	29.0	29.3
Land systems	21.0	17.5	18.2	19.6	19.9	18.7
Air systems	36.7	34.7	32.7	32.4	33.0	31.9

Source: UK Defence Statistics, op. cit., Table 1.4.

and the continued orientation of its forces towards aerospace. As the EH.101 helicopter moves into production, and as Eurofighter 2000 production follows the Tornado upgrade programme, this commitment to aerospace seems likely to be maintained.

UK-expressed interest in the Tomahawk cruise missile is a reflection of the MoD's continued orientation towards high technology and of a growing interest in precision-strike weapons. Also relevant is the UK's growing if cautious interest in ballistic missile defence.[14] However, because of changes in 1992–3 to the classification scheme for research, development and production spending, it is not clear whether the UK government seeks to maintain the British capacity to develop and produce such weapons. Over the period since 1975–6, it is apparent that the tendency has been to spend less and less of the equipment budget on research and development (see Table 5). Private British corporate investment in defence R&D is also diminishing.[15]

14. See, for instance, 'Britain to consider need for high-tech anti-missile defence', *Independent*, 16 Feb. 1994.
15. 'Industry R&D spending falls in the UK', *Jane's Defence Weekly*, 8 Jan. 1994.

Table 5: Share of equipment procurement expenditure allocated to Research and Development

Year	%	Year	%
1975–6	32.3	1989–90	24.1
1980–81	30.6	1990–91	23.7
1985–6	25.2	1991–2	23.6
1988–9	23.8	1992–3	20.6

Source: UK Defence Statistics, op. cit., Table 1.4.

Manpower and force structure

In July 1990, as noted above, the British government announced its Options for Change initiative, which comprised proposed changes in the national force structure to reflect the end of the Cold War. There was pressure in the country for some kind of peace dividend and for evidence that the MoD was thinking positively about the opportunities which the new global situation presented. The central Options for Change choices were kept in place despite the Kuwait crisis, and further thinking led to some additional cuts in planned manning levels. There were no substantial changes made either after NATO's choice of a new force structure in the spring of 1991 or after its acceptance of the New Strategic Concept in November 1991.

Under Options for Change, most significant was that the army's manpower was to be cut by one-third. Instead of keeping three divisions in Germany plus one in reserve in the UK, the British army was to have one armoured division in Germany with a mechanized division being kept in the UK for movement to the continent in the event of crisis. Instead of a British corps in Germany, there was to be a British division in the eight- or nine-division Allied Rapid Reaction Corps. Britain's specialist forces, in particular the 3rd Commando Brigade and the UK contribution to the ACE Mobile Force, were left unchanged. The Royal Air Force presence in Germany was to be cut from four air bases to two and from 12 front-line squadrons to six. At sea, Britain's submarine force was to be cut drastically (from 27 to around 16)[16] and the projected number of destroyers and frigates to be deployed was cut from 'around 50' to 'around 40' (which many would have said was a more realistic procurement target even in 1988).

Given that Britain was keeping its three 'Harrier Carriers', it was apparent that forces with clear out-of-area capabilities were relatively protected, although the fleet target has since been further cut to 35 frigates and destroyers. There were, however, many debates about the army cuts, with emotional objections to the mergers/abolition of some regiments, but also calculations that the army had simply been left with insufficient units to cover its responsibilities, which encompass man-power-intensive Northern Ireland and UN duties including service in former Yugoslavia.[17]

Under Options for Change, Britain decided to change slightly the balance of its ground forces from armoured to lighter units and could thus be seen to be moving implicitly towards a greater emphasis on intervention and peacekeeping forces. The original cuts involved moving from 55 to 38 infantry battalions (a cut of 32 per cent) and from 19 to 11 armoured regiments (a cut of 42 per cent).[18] Two basic considerations need to be noted here. The first is that Britain did not hesitate on the issue of stationing forces in Germany after the unification of the country. It opted quickly for a reduced but substantial presence, including an armoured division. This was politically favoured because a pull-out from Germany would have signalled a substantial move towards the renationalization of defence in Europe. In terms of military organization, it would have meant that Britain's army would have had to be cut back much further: even during the Cold War, Britain had judged that the UK mainland could be protected by around 100,000 men, a mix of regular and reserve soldiers. The British involvement in Germany, through the Allied Rapid Reaction Corps which the UK commands, guaranteed that the British army would remain sizeable in

16. By 1994 the target was a force of 12 nuclear attack submarines.
17. First Britain had a hospital field unit of about 250 people with the UN force in Croatia. It then deployed over 2,400 troops to protect humanitarian aid going to Bosnia.
18. 'Army under fire over the Bosnia effect', *Daily Telegraph*, 29 Sept. 1992.

terms of men and equipment. A second factor is that Britain has had to find substantial light forces for duties in Northern Ireland. In terms of the harsh logic of justifying force sizes to meet commitments, about one-third of the army's personnel are justified by Northern Ireland duties. The UK deploys up to 13,000 regular troops there and, given the demands of training troops before they go and providing them with a respite afterwards, some 30–40,000 troops, many of them infantrymen, have Northern Ireland-related duties at any one time. Although the number of infantry battalions has been increased to 40, doubts remain about the army's capacity to meet the demands on it as long as its duties in Northern Ireland remain substantial. However, the IRA announced a ceasefire at the end of August 1994, and if the conflict were settled, the British army could in principle be further cut by at least 20 per cent. Certainly the Treasury would press for additional cuts in the defence budget.

In July 1994 the Ministry of Defence announced further amendments to its expenditure and employment when it revealed the findings of its *Front Line First* study. The changes revealed in the study were not seen as constituting a review of defence policy, but as supportive of the long-standing policy of the Ministry to spend money as effectively as possible. Thus the changes were not to damage the capabilities of Britain's front-line forces, but they did involve considerable job cuts in both the military and civilian sections of the MoD. The Royal Air Force, much of whose engineering work was to be transferred to civilian contractors, took the largest cuts. Overall, the Royal Navy and Royal Marines were to be reduced by 4.1 per cent (1,900 jobs), the army by 1.9 per cent (2,200 jobs), the Royal Air Force by 11.6 per cent personnel (7,500 jobs) and MoD civilian employees by 6.5 per cent (7,100 jobs). These changes came on top of the major personnel reductions in UK services introduced since the late 1980s (see Table 6) and the number of Royal Air Force employees will fall to 64,500, compared with 91,000 in 1989. However, the changes had at least some significant policy implications: in particular, they were based on the plan that the RAF would close one of its two remaining bases in Germany, and the commitment to greater inter-service integration (or 'jointery', as it is known), included the creation of a 20,000-strong

Table 6: Changing personnel strengths of UK armed forces ('000s)

	1989	1990	1991	1992	1993	1994
All services	311.6	305.7	298.1	293.4	274.8	254.5
Royal Navy and Marines	64.6	63.2	62.1	62.1	59.4	55.8
Army	155.6	152.8	147.6	145.4	134.6	123.0
Royal Air Force	91.4	89.7	88.4	86.0	80.9	75.7

Source: UK Defence Statistics, op. cit., Table 2.7.

Rapid Deployment Force linking 5 Airborne Brigade (two battalions of the Parachute Regiment and two line infantry battalions), 24 Air Mobile Brigade, the 3 Royal Marine Commando Brigade, and RAF aircraft with other logistical support.

Overall the MoD calculated that the changes identified would save £750 million a year from 1996–7. It will not be apparent for some time whether all the anticipated reforms, covering base closures, more joint service training, contracting improvements, the reorganization of research, the movement of engineering work, especially from the RAF, to industry, and so on, will actually be successful,[19] nor is it clear how much of its savings the ministry will be allowed to keep.

Equipment plans and procurement

British equipment plans have not been reshaped drastically in quality or variety by the end of the Cold War since the intention stands to deploy well-equipped, high-technology, balanced forces. The government envisages procuring some items in fewer numbers (most obviously tanks) but has not cancelled major projects. As elsewhere in Europe, projects have been delayed and slowed, but they have not been abandoned. Thus the Eurofighter 2000, the EH.101, ASRAAM, the Challenger 2, MLRS and, of course, Trident, remain in the UK programme.

19. See, for instance, 'MoD yet to finalise plan to curb research spending', *The Financial Times*, 18 July 1994.

On the other hand, there has understandably been no rush into new projects, and caution is particularly apparent with regard to an anti-tank helicopter and a new transport helicopter for the British army. Should the British decide not to opt for the Tiger in the anti-tank role (or should the Germans and French cancel the Tiger), they would probably lose interest in the Trigat anti-tank missiles. Britain has also lost any sense of urgency or commitment with regard to a stand-off missile to replace its free-fall WE.177 nuclear bombs. The choice was broadly between developing a system with France or buying something from the US, but Britain looks unlikely to opt for either in the foreseeable future.

In terms of procurement techniques, Britain remains committed to using competitive tendering as much as possible, and in principle will consider bids from the continent, the US and even the wider world. It has, for instance, bought the Tucano trainer from Brazil for its air force, although the aircraft is being made under licence in Northern Ireland by Shorts. The government argues that the 90 per cent of procurement contracts which are won by British firms are won on merit. Britain also favours collaborative programmes which involve competition for as many of the contracts as possible. Even if the programme must use a monopoly national champion (such as BAe for combat aircraft), competitive tendering is sought for subcontracts. Given Britain's commitment to competition, it is clearly no champion of the principle of *juste retour* in procurement.[20] Britain is, however, not anxious to see Article 223 of the Rome Treaty abandoned, perhaps partly because it needs freedom in some special defence areas (most obviously the nuclear sector), and it is also wary of the impact on transatlantic relations of the greater involvement of the European Commission with defence generally.

As shown by the extensive list of projects published each year in the MoD's *Statement on the Defence Estimates* (*SDE*), Britain's commitment to collaborative projects is significant and probably increasing. Its commitment to the Eurofighter remains unshaken, despite its delay,

20. 'Juste retour' is the idea that states participating in collaborative projects should be allocated work in proportion to the share of the costs of the project which they bear. A state planning to buy 40% of the initial production of a system would get 40% of development and production work.

modification and cost escalation problems. The EH.101 anti-submarine and transport helicopter is another major collaborative project. Collaboration is a tradition in British aerospace procurement, but commitment to the Horizon frigate project with France (and to a lesser extent Italy) shows collaboration moving to ships as well. Britain remains interested in securing access to US technology through collaborative projects as well as off-the-shelf purchases, and the *SDEs* show a significant number of projects with the US as a partner.[21] However, few such projects involve much genuine joint development and for a range of reasons, transatlantic collaborative research or even development work rarely leads to production. West Europeans are accepted in British industry and government as easier to collaborate with.

British official thinking on the defence industrial base is guarded and perhaps limited. Thus the Ministry of Defence refuses to accept that it should fund the development of the proposed Future Large Aircraft because of the beneficial impact on Europe's aerospace industry. The Conservative governments in office since 1979 have argued that state intervention in the economy should be minimal and that the state is poorly placed to identify key commercial technologies or strategic industries. They have also felt that the UK would have little difficulty in buying most types of military equipment in the global market place: indeed, in the mid-1980s the UK could identify only four sorts of military equipment which could not be imported. Finally, during the Cold War it anticipated that any war would have to be fought at short notice with existing equipment rather than with items rushed into production. Thus the British government is reluctant to accept that the country's defence industrial capability is an asset for its front-line forces.

However, the Falklands conflict and to a much greater extent the Kuwait war illustrated that UK armed forces did in fact benefit substantially from help from industry. The MoD is being pressed to think harder about industrial base issues as reduced contracts drive more

---

21. The *Statement on the Defence Estimates* 1994 (p. 63) lists 22 collaborative projects in the production or service stage. The US is a partner in six of these and France and Germany in eight. There are 21 projects listed as in development, and the US is involved is 11, Germany in 12, and France in 16.

suppliers out of business, but there is little sign of a coherent policy emerging. The Ministry of Defence is being rather more open than formerly with the defence industry about its long-term procurement plans, but it has no overt line on the sorts of defence industrial capability which it wants to maintain in the UK. Policy tends to be made 'on the hoof', as it had to be when Westland almost went bankrupt in 1985–6 and when the scope for UK-based competition in defence electronics was eroded by the GEC-Siemens takeover of Plessey and the near-collapse of Ferranti at the end of the 1980s. Britain has allowed foreign firms, particularly Thomson-CSF, to buy into the country's defence industry, but British security clearance rules and practices make it hard for firms to integrate their activities on a truly transnational basis.

Domestic political considerations

In introducing Options for Change, the Ministry of Defence was clearly anxious to stress at an early stage that it was not trapped by antiquated thinking and was ready to adapt to the transformed world. However, if 'Options' was designed to head off future pressure for defence cuts, it was clearly unsuccessful and constantly downward revisions to the defence budget have been pressed for and secured.

Pressure has come more from within government than from public opinion as a whole. The launch of *Front Line First* reflected the fact that the post-Cold War development of British defence policy has been driven by two conceptually separate debates conducted mainly within Whitehall. One concerns the question of the defence capabilities which Britain should have after the Cold War. The other focuses on the extent to which the MoD wastes money and thus should be pushed to improve its practices by having its budget cut. The Treasury appears consistently to have asserted that waste in the MoD is considerable and that budget cuts need not mean capability cuts. *Front Line First* represents the MoD's effort to demonstrate to the rest of the government – indeed to Britain's politically active groups as a whole – that it is putting its house in order, and that future defence budget cuts will therefore have to mean reduced capabilities.

The government appears to have concluded that defence as such is not a major concern of public opinion and that the public's principal concern is unemployment. As in July 1994, when it combined its announcement of 18,000 job cuts with details of new contracts to be placed, the government clearly signalled that it feared many would judge its changes mainly by their impact on the employment position.

There are a number of politically active groups pressing for defence efforts to be maintained. Within the Conservative Party, the army and navy have traditional supporters who firmly oppose cuts in the number of combat units. The cross-party House of Commons Defence Committee is an advocate of sturdy British defence efforts even after the Cold War and, despite having a Conservative chairman, it has regularly criticized the government's defence cuts. As formal policy, the Labour Party would like to see British defence spending fall to the West European average share of GDP, but this is in itself a falling target and the unemployment which its attainment would entail would be very difficult for most of the Labour Party to accept. Concern with what other West Europeans are doing is a likely consideration to some in the Conservative Party, who are increasingly loath to see Britain do more than its share when other, richer states do considerably less.

Overall, however, Members of Parliament are poorly informed on defence questions, and the general public too has little interest. There is little public familiarity with such issues as the size of the defence budget, the amount it has been cut to date, its size in relation to spending on health, education or social security and so on. Thus British public opinion is not a major constraint on the government as far as defence cuts are concerned, at least within the bounds which the government is considering. Perhaps understandably, the government seems content with this situation and does little to encourage serious debate on British security and defence policy in the parliament or outside. Interestingly, in presenting *Front Line First*, the Defence Minister made far more of the job cuts and contracts that of the innovation of a 20,000-man, joint service Rapid Deployment Force. The implication was either that the force was to bring little increase in capability, or that the government did not want to encourage speculation about the circumstances in which it might be deployed or the frequency with which such circumstances might arise.

Defence and multilateral commitments

The British government sees NATO as the cornerstone of West European security and would see itself as a committed member, taking seriously NATO's force planning structures and goals. Back in 1955 Britain's treaty commitment to maintain substantial forces in Germany was a gesture to permit Germany to join the Western European Union and NATO. The British Army of the Rhine long dominated the shape of the British army, and Britain's NATO responsibilities in the North Atlantic led it to build and sustain a blue-water navy oriented towards anti-submarine warfare. Britain's nuclear policy has, of course, had a strong national dimension but it has deployed its nuclear weapons in Germany and it has won West European acceptance that its strategic nuclear forces make a contribution to the defence of Western Europe as a whole.

British defence capabilities are thus very much oriented towards alliance needs and this will continue to be the case in future. As the *SDE* 1992 notes explicitly, Britain does not want to see the renationalization of defence in Europe. On the operational level, the Kuwait war brought home the need for sustained fighting capabilities and the value of inter-operability. The UK is therefore looking for cooperation with allies to reinforce these factors.

Special considerations apply in the nuclear area where traditionally the British government has stressed (especially to the domestic audience) that the UK possesses an independent nuclear deterrent. Yet Britain argues that its nuclear forces are also a contribution to NATO security as a whole, not least because they involve a second centre of decision-making and British warheads are included in NATO targeting plans. Looking forward, Britain will be pressed towards closer contact with France in particular, and for three reasons. First, pressures could well grow for both countries to join strategic nuclear disarmament negotiations and they would benefit from being able to adopt a common stance in such talks.

Second, both will need to be able to explain the roles of their nuclear weapons in a disarming world where nuclear non-proliferation is being attempted. Should they offer different answers, the credibility of both responses is likely to be reduced (and equipment cooperation hindered). Finally, the possibility that the US might withdraw from Europe gives more salience to the issue of how British and French forces alone could protect other parts of Europe as well as their own territories. French leaders have been more willing than their British counterparts to recognize this publicly as an issue but have not to date generated answers. These factors together provide some foundation for a greater British willingness to talk to Paris on nuclear matters.

Summary and conclusion

Britain is strongly oriented to maintaining a coalition basis for its defence. It would prefer that basis to be NATO but recognizes that the West European grouping will become more prominent and may eventually take the lead. Its commitment to such a coalition basis reflects the belief that its collapse would be a disaster for the region, including the UK, and that the UK will lack the capacity for even limited military intervention outside the NATO area without external help. It is particularly aware of the transport, communications, logistics and intelligence assets needed for many intervention activities, assets which the US can make available and which West Europeans could build for themselves only at great expense.

However, Britain identifies the defence of its homeland as a separate if not explicitly higher priority than the defence of allies, and wishes to retain a high degree of ultimate autonomy in the defence and security policy area. As regards external intervention, Britain could be regarded as simultaneously cautious and assertive. It can be assertive about commitments where there is a clear military goal which can be achieved with a short, if intense period of military activity. On the other hand, not least because of its Northern Irish experience, it is cautious about possibly protracted involvement in conflicts where the military have a peacekeeping/policing role.

There is thus some paradox in British policy. Although it is among the more cautious of European states with regard to proposals for the integration of defence in the framework of the European Union, Britain endorses the general goal of enhancing the effectiveness of Europe's defence effort. Moreover, the practical steps taken to remodel Britain's force structure could fairly be said to be well suited to the discharge of the tasks which European security, broadly defined, seems likely to require.

However, major questions hang over the future of British defence policy. In particular, there are widespread doubts whether the envisaged sources of savings, either from the improved practices promoted since 1983 or the *Front Line First* study, will in fact succeed in making available the money needed for effective operational capability. Certainly the National Audit Office finds that MoD procurement remains flawed despite all the attention it has received. In the early 1990s Philip Sabin anticipated that Britain would not for long be able to maintain balanced forces with a capability for high-intensity warfare and global policing using a declining defence budget.[22] A modern, well-trained navy with blue-water capability, an army with significant heavy armour, a powerful air force and strategic nuclear forces seem likely to require increased rather than lower defence spending, despite the efficiency measures of *Front Line First*. The changes introduced since Sabin wrote have not dissipated the weight of analysis, and many fears remain that Britain will deploy forces which increasingly are inadequately trained and equipped.

Perhaps the major weakness of the British approach is that it has not addressed overtly what sort of military role Britain ought to play in the world. The Ministry of Defence recognizes that this is at heart a foreign and security policy question and thus one for the Foreign and Commonwealth Office in the first place and the government as a whole in the final analysis. The MoD can make only broad statements such as that appearing early in the *Front Line First* report:

22. Philip Sabin, 'British defence choices beyond "Options for Change"', *International Affairs*, vol. 69, no. 2, April 1993, especially pp. 279ff.

Our armed forces provide a crucial underpinning to our foreign and security policies. They not only enable us to defend the United Kingdom and our Dependent Territories, but also ensure that the UK can speak and act with authority, knowing that, if necessary, we can enforce our rights and contribute to maintaining international stability in Europe and more widely.[23]

One point of British difficulty is, of course, that what Britain would be prepared to do will depend in part on what its EU partners and the US are also prepared to contribute, but the present British stance does not make it seem well prepared for the 1996 European Intergovernmental Conference which is to address common security and defence policy matters.[24]

23. *Front Line First*, op. cit., p. 5. For a similar lack of precision, see the speech of Malcolm Rifkind, the Defence Minister, at King's College, London on 15 February 1994. He defined one of five choices of British policy 'as an active commitment to the United Nations and its concept of global security, as well as to other international organisations promoting security in its widest sense. This is coupled with active engagement in international affairs on a world-wide basis, as a result of extensive commercial and trading interests as well as historical and emotional ties to Commonwealth and other states, often with substantial expatriate communities. All this was encapsulated in Douglas Hurd's description of the United Kingdom as a "medium sized power with a well-developed sense of international responsibility".' (Text provided by Ministry of Defence.)
24. For an editorial arguing that British forces are overstretched in terms of the demands on them and in need of a formal defence review which would analyse explicitly the threats to British interests, see 'Time for a defence review', *The Financial Times*, 11 July 1994.

7 CONCLUSION

Trevor Taylor

Approach and setting

The defence policies of West European states have been much affected by four major developments since the late 1980s. First, and most important, the Soviet Union abandoned control of the European states which it had dominated since 1945. The Moscow-based conventional military threat to Western Europe has consequently disappeared. Second, the movement towards European integration recognized that defence cannot be separated from other areas of inter-governmental cooperation. At Maastricht it was accepted that a common foreign and security policy would on occasions involve armed forces and that defence cooperation in (Western) Europe should be handled for the time being by a strengthened, Brussels-based WEU. Third, the Kuwait crisis, followed by the violent disintegration of Yugoslavia, emphasized that the end of the Cold War did not mean the end of violent conflict. The demand for intervention forces of one sort or another is rising, as the increased number of UN peacekeeping operations indicates.[1] Finally, the recession in the developed world as a whole in the early 1990s prompted governments to reduce their budget deficits by cutting defence spending. The impact of national economic difficulties on defence efforts was significant.

The Maastricht Treaty indicated that, while NATO was seen as the central organization for West European security, the members of the European Union aspired to cooperate even more closely on defence in a WEU/EC context than they ever had in NATO. Maastricht referred

---

1. The UN mounted 13 peacekeeping operations between 1945 and 1988, and a further 15 operations from then until the beginning of 1993.

to a common defence policy leading eventually to 'a common defence'. Yet there were fears expressed at a high political level that defence could become renationalized after the extensive external threat to Western Europe had disappeared. It is clear that political leaders in France, Germany and the United Kingdom, for instance, conceived that European integration could unravel, not least because countries go their own way on defence issues.[2]

The basic thrust of this project was to ascertain whether, after the Cold War, the key states of Western Europe were moving closer together in their defence policies or whether they were growing apart. Such an enquiry clearly raised methodological issues. Of special importance was the way in which growing together/growing apart was to be measured. A common set of issues, which served as a basis for the national chapters at the heart of this study, represented an explicit but clearly subjective and thus debatable set of key factors.

The project did not only address the issue of whether states are or are not moving closer together on defence matters. It also considered some important factors which will make drawing together more or less difficult. These included not only the general philosophical orientation of governments towards foreign policy, the use of force, nuclear weapons and so on, but also the different structures of defence decision- and policy-making in national capitals.

World views, defence roles and NATO

Although the precise formulation varies from state to state, the five states under review here stress that their defence forces will make contributions at three levels:

- the defence of national territory, including any overseas possessions;
- the defence of allies, mainly in NATO/WEU; and

2. See, for instance, the introduction to the British Defence White Paper, *Statement on the Defence Estimates 1992*, by the Secretary of State for Defence.

- the maintenance of security and order beyond Europe in the world as a whole.

Britain, France and the Netherlands differ from Germany and Italy in still having overseas defence responsibilities for colonial territories. These territories, not protected under the NATO or WEU treaties, can be seen as requiring the three states concerned to maintain balanced forces for their defence and to limit the extent to which they may become involved in force specialization cooperative activities with partners.

In the longer term, there must be concern that formal stress on the defence of national territory, as in the British Defence White Papers, could contribute to the renationalization of defence, especially as regards land forces. If the risks from Moscow continue to diminish, there must also be a danger, especially if countries rarely participate in external multilateral intervention activities to support international order, that their armed forces will be seen as too large for the defence of national territory only.

There are many similarities in the basic security and defence policy thinking emerging from the five states under study. In particular, there is acceptance of the need to protect against the residual threat from Russia and of the increasing demand for peacekeeping and other intervention forces in the wider world. All also accept a continuing role for NATO and the value of a US commitment to and presence in Europe. There is less agreement on the details of the NATO role.

France and Germany are probably not ready to tolerate what is seen as US domination of NATO. Since Germany is the main host for US forces, other European members of NATO have accepted, with greater or lesser reluctance, that there should be a more coherent and effective West European voice in NATO. A West European caucus there, previously rejected as potentially divisive, seems to have been accepted as desirable at Rome and Maastricht in 1991.

However there is no apparent consensus, even within West European states, about the terms under which a US presence in Europe would be maintained in the mid-1990s and after. Two key questions on which West Europeans might seek to develop agreed judgments are:

- will the US remain interested in NATO if it is a partner rather than a dominant player in the alliance? and
- if the alliance had a much lower political profile than that which it enjoyed during the Cold War, would US commitment to NATO be maintained?

Germany's government is the only one that has worked up any enthusiasm about widening NATO's membership, most obviously to Central European states. Defence Minister Volker Rühe has been most associated with this position, with Foreign Minister Klaus Kinkel providing less enthusiastic backing. Most European governments, however, are probably ready to accept a wider NATO provided the timing and approach are right, which means that the minimum reaction is generated in Moscow, the decision is endorsed by national legislatures including the US Senate, and the new NATO members can make a contribution to European security rather than simply being consumers of it.

No West European state wants NATO formally to take on a general out-of-area role beyond that agreed with regard to CSCE and UN peacekeeping forces. Given the disagreements between the US and Europeans on out-of-area questions in the past, forcing such matters to be addressed in NATO would probably mean giving intra-allied disputes more prominence. The Netherlands and Britain, however, are most ready to contemplate 'NATO labels' being put on out-of-area actions on an ad hoc basis, when the US and Europeans are working together. France resists such developments, seeing them as too big an opportunity for the US to spread its influence. However, France's apparent readiness to attend the Defence Planning Committee when peacekeeping is discussed should makes it easier for NATO to coordinate preparations in such areas as command and control, logistics support, infrastructure, training and exercises.[3]

On the maintenance of order on a global scale, which essentially is drawn from foreign policy positions, the European Union rather than

3. See para. 4 of the DPC Final Communiqué of 11 Dec. 1992, M-DPC-2(92)102, NATO Press Service, Brussels.

NATO would appear to be the logical foundation for European action. NATO's proud boast has always been that it is a defensive alliance geared essentially to the effective, collective protection of its members against external attack. Foreign policy cooperation has been needed in NATO as a peripheral matter, on the grounds that the collective defence commitments of NATO would lose credibility if its members were constantly squabbling on other issues. On the other hand, the development of a common foreign and security policy has become a central, treaty-based aspect of the European Union, and Maastricht provided a clear if abstract framework for future developments: the European Union is to have a CFSP and, when that policy acquires a defence dimension (i.e. when defence ministries get involved), activities involving armed forces will be handled by the WEU. The operation of such a mechanism in practice remains open to doubt, as was shown by the decreased coherence of the Community over Kuwait once questions of contributions to fighting moved to the top of the agenda. Moreover, much needs to be done in the WEU Council and its military planning cell before the organization has much military credibility. The fundamental design may yet lead to the European Union having policy without capabilities, and NATO having capabilities but not policy.

In addition the different political cultures in EU states influence their readiness to intervene. The German Socialist Democratic Party (SPD) does not regard a mandate for military action based on a European Union CFSP as adequate and it is ready to contemplate German involvement only in UN-mandated actions.[4] The Netherlands and Italy also have a strong preference for a UN mandate before they act militarily, but Britain and France would not be willing to give the Security Council a veto over their military intervention activities.

4.   The SPD has rejected the coalition CDU/CSU/FDP proposal for a constitutional change which would allow Germany to take part in collective self-defence operations outside the UN framework, provided that they are carried out with other countries in the framework of alliances and other regional agreements to which Germany belongs. The coalition has also proposed that Germany should be empowered to take part in UN Security Council-mandated peacekeeping and peacemaking operations. 'Bonn agreed formula for joining UN forces', *The Financial Times*, 14 Jan. 1993.

faultel

The position on issues of global and regional order is complex. On the one hand, there are differences between national political cultures and traditions: for instance, it might be felt that Germany and the Netherlands are generally more reluctant than France or Britain to conclude that the use of force may be needed. On the other hand, differences within states among political parties can also be substantial. The differences in Germany between the SPD and the Christian Democratic Union (CDU) are clear. In the early 1990s the Gaullist opposition in France felt the socialist government was spending too little on defence. In Britain, the socialist and liberal democrat parties have tended to argue that the government has not done enough to promote international order, for instance in former Yugoslavia, although in office they could prove just as cautious as the Conservatives. Overall, the chances of achieving consensus in Western Europe will depend much on the coincidence of the most recent electoral results in EU states. Finally, it needs to be stressed that what can arise in the EU may not be some differences of hard national interest, but honestly conflicting judgments of what policy instruments will work best in a situation and what risks are acceptable: in January 1991 there were still differences within and among the states in coalition against Iraq as to whether sanctions should be given more time to work.

These problems and differences may well press EU governments to restrict common foreign and security policies to agreement on desired goals. Yet such policies will lack significance and credibility unless account is also taken of the resources available to attain the target, the tactics to be used, and the risks to be taken. These matters lead to questions about where leadership and initiative are to come from in the European Union. Such leadership will have to address established, fundamental questions in international politics about the divisibility of peace and the viability of an order for some specific region (such as the Middle East) without some wider global basis. The place of armed force in the maintenance of regional and global order is a subject on which West Europeans vary in their views, and further debate is needed to secure agreement on some basic principles.

Preoccupations in the European Union states vary with regard to regions beyond Western Europe. The southern EU countries are most sensitive to developments in the Mediterranean while Germany's focus is on Eastern Europe and the former Soviet Union. However, there are some factors which moderate the impact of these concerns. First, all West European states share a dependence on Middle East oil. Second, as far as military intervention is concerned, there are many parts of Eastern Europe where Germany could not contribute, given its view that the Bundeswehr cannot be sent to areas occupied by the Wehrmacht in the Second World War. Third, France is both a northern and a southern European power and Britain has a tradition of a military presence in the Mediterranean.

In considering the contributions of defence ministries to international order, there are two specific ideas which might have helped with previous intervention activities and which merit further reflection. One is that it should be accepted from the outset that a legitimate function of action against an aggressor government is to punish that government, preferably the individuals concerned. Action need not be restricted to exercising the pressure required to retrieve what has been 'stolen' by the aggressor. Unless there is clear punishment, other potential aggressors may be tempted to see what they can get away with. This argument has relevance for both the Iraq–Kuwait crisis and the Yugoslav crisis.

The other is that, while terms of art should be retained for certain sorts of missions (such as observers, peacemaking, peacekeeping, humanitarian relief), the planning of such interventions should build into even initial calculations the possibility, even the likelihood, that one sort of force may need to change into another. Those delivering humanitarian relief should if possible have extra protection, deployed perhaps over the horizon, which can come to their aid and prevent their being used as hostages. Observers should not be sent if there is no potential to take further action in the light of what they observe.

Burden-sharing

An important element of possible convergence in Europe is financial and concerns the extent to which the different West European states are contributing in an equitable and appropriate way to the overall defence effort. Burden-sharing has been a much-debated issue in NATO, with no single indicator being regarded as satisfactory. However, if a series of indicators is taken as a bundle, and the question is whether the differences among countries are widening or narrowing, at least two contrasting hypotheses can be considered plausible. One asserts that, at a time when West Europeans are openly expressing aspirations to a common defence policy, the indicators of their defence effort could be expected to converge rather than diverge. The other anticipates that, when the central threat has disappeared and the future needs for armed forces have become much more uncertain, the key factors which had pressed countries towards a similar level of effort have gone: greater discrepancies will then be expected as countries produce differing judgments on to how best to cope with the new situation.

The figures drawn from NATO sources and presented in Tables 1, 2 and 3 indicate that the second hypothesis has more weight. Table 1 shows how the five states covered in this volume changed their defence spending in real terms and without taking into account exchange-rate fluctuations between 1989 and 1993. There is clearly a wide range of responses.

In terms of defence spending measured in national currencies, France and Italy clearly responded differently from Germany, the Netherlands and the UK to the end of the Cold War. This difference is not related to economic performance since, in the 1989–92/3 period, the Dutch had the best economic performance and yet cut defence the most. Even omitting Germany with its special features resulting from unification, the deviation from the mean of countries' per caput spending on defence increased markedly after 1989. Moreover, despite the general tendency to spend a smaller percentage of GDP on defence, the deviations from the mean also widened after 1988, even when German figures are omitted. The major countries of Western Europe appear to be moving away rather than towards either a standard amount per caput to be spent on defence, or a standard share of GDP being allocated to defence.

All five countries are looking forward eventually to a period of stable defence expenditure, starting at the latest towards the end of the 1990s.

Table 1: Change in real national defence spending in local currency values (%)

Country	Change between 1989 and 1993
France	−3.1
Germany	−14.3
Italy	−5.9*
Netherlands	−12.0
United Kingdom	−11.8
Average change	−9.4

*Figures relate only to the 1989–92 period.
Source: Derived from Table 1 of 'Financial and economic data relating to NATO defence', *NATO Review*, April 1994.

Table 2: Change in defence spending's share of GDP (%)

Country	1988	1989	1991	1992	1993
France	3.8	3.7	3.6	3.4	3.4
Germany	2.9	2.8	2.2	2.0	2.0
Italy	2.3	2.3	2.1	2.0	n/a
Netherlands	3.0	2.8	2.5	2.5	2.3
United Kingdom	4.2	4.1	4.3	4.0	3.8
Average change	3.2	3.1	2.9	2.8	n/a

Source: Derived from Table 3 of 'Financial and economic data', op. cit.

Table 3: Movements in per caput GDP and defence expenditure, 1989–93 (in 1985 $US)

Country	GDP per caput in 1989	GDP per caput in 1993	% change	Defence exp. per caput in 1989	Defence exp. per caput in 1993	% change
France	10,529	10,646	+1.1	385	365	−5.2
Germany	11,096	10,251	−6.3	315	209	−34.7
Italy*	8,391	8,702	+3.7	180	168	−6.7
Netherlands	9,597	10,024	+4.4	278	238	−14.4
United Kingdom	9,178	9,011	−1.2	375	326	−13.1

*Figures relate only to the 1989–92 period.
Source: Derived from Table 4 of 'Financial and economic data', op. cit.

Meanwhile, apart from in France the trend is for more cuts, which seem to be driven as much by the recession and a reduced tax revenue base for governments as by a diminished sense of danger. Britain and Germany, in the autumn of 1992 and on several occasions since, changed their defence spending plans to bring in further reductions, while the Netherlands did so in early 1993. Italy hopes to increase its defence spending but, given the country's wider economic problems and its history of low defence expenditure, this seems unlikely. Only in France is there a clear effort to sustain defence spending, especially on equipment.

At a time when there is no significant, immediate threat to give shape to defence policy, but instead there are more remote dangers and a seemingly limitless demand for intervention forces, some informal indicators may gain favour with defence (and even finance) ministries seeking to control the fall in their budget. Some such possible guides are:

• maintain real spending at an agreed level (which some states hope to do in the late 1990s); or
• maintain defence as a fixed share of GDP (which may have particular appeal in France); or
• maintain defence spending in cash terms but do not allow for inflation (Germany at one stage planned to spend DM50 billion per year on defence but has now fallen below even this figure); or
• increase or decrease defence spending by a given percentage each year, as the 1977 NATO '3 per cent' commitment sought to do.

These four criteria seek to identify some sense of what it is reasonable to spend on defence in an uncertain world, but there are few signs of national governments in Western Europe either settling on any one of them or even adjusting their defence spending in close consultation with allies. Defence ministries broadly inform allies as to the outcome of their arguments with their finance ministries, but in contrast to the '3 per cent' commitment developed in NATO in late 1977 and 1978 when the threat was increasing, there has been no equivalent principle agreed to guide defence cuts in a time of reduced threat. Informal consultations among governments do not appear to give much attention to defence spending levels or to changing national force structures, as Paragraph 9 of the DPC December 1993 Communiqué hinted.[5]

These matters raise certain questions for governments in future. Can European governments achieve the cooperation targeted in the Maastricht Treaty if there is growing diversity of defence effort? Will West European governments be any more successful than NATO governments were in developing indicators with which to address the burden-sharing issue? Could a category of 'international security expenditure' be developed which could include foreign aid as well as defence spending? Will West European governments be inclined to consult more, even on an informal basis, on their defence expenditure plans? In the event of funding shortages hitting equipment levels and training in national armed forces, will multinational units such as the Franco-German Corps and the Anglo-Dutch amphibious force receive favoured protection?

Force structures

All countries are adjusting their force structures to reflect the end of the Cold War but the degree of consultation with allies varies, as does the progress countries have made in this area.

- *Britain* has made most progress, with its Options for Change programme well into the implementation stage.
- *Germany* has agreed that its armed forces will not exceed 340,000 but it seems hard to justify such large forces in the longer term, especially given German reservations about military intervention activities. A further German restructuring exercise must be expected now that Russian troops have left Germany and the Bundeswehr has been reduced to 370,000 from its height of more than 500,000 when East Germany forces were first absorbed.

5. Para. 9 read in part: 'A number of planned national force reductions will have an effect on the future size and capabilities of main defence forces, and we initiated a review of the implications of changing force levels for the new force structure.' DPC Communiqué, op. cit.

- *The Netherlands* announced in January 1993 that it would reduce its forces from their current level of 125,000 to around 70,000 at the turn of the century.
- *Italy*'s debate on its force structure, as on other aspects of its defence policy, has reached no positive conclusion. The latest government proposal is to reduce the armed forces by about one-third, with the army in particular being cut by 40 per cent.
- More information is available on *France*'s equipment spending than its force structure plans.

A fundamental issue in four of the five states under scrutiny is whether to maintain conscription. Active national debates are under way everywhere, but of the five states covered here only the Netherlands has taken a positive decision to abolish it. Problems with conscription include the inequity of calling up only a small proportion of the people who are eligible because of the need for a smaller force structure; the limited training which can be carried out in the short conscription periods (12 months or less) now in force, at a time when states need flexible, well-trained forces; and the political difficulties of sending conscripts even on peacekeeping missions where they will be in some danger. Sending only conscripts who volunteer for such missions may help with this problem, but it means that special units have to be formed rather than existing units being sent. The shortcomings of conscription make it a reasonable prediction that it will have been abolished in the European Union states by the end of the century unless some states retain military service as one element in a much wider 'community service' scheme.

Many West European countries recognize that they will continue to come under pressure to provide forces for deployment outside the NATO area and accordingly are seeking to establish rapid deployment force elements in their services. Most of these efforts are national, although the established Anglo-Dutch amphibious brigade and the planned Franco-German Corps might be considered to fall within this category. However, national efforts are not aimed at self-sufficiency but implicitly rely on others for some needs, such as air or sea transport, reconnaissance, air cover, and command, control and communications.

Some important questions concern the overlaps and gaps in overall WEU capabilities which may be established as a result of force restructuring. As far as out-of-area or intervention forces are concerned, Western Europe will have a collection of national (and multinational) units with some specialized amphibious and airborne capabilities, sea-based fixed-wing aircraft and transport assets. Whether the whole will add up to more or to less than the sum of its parts will depend on adjustments to force structures which could be made in the light of the efforts of others. There are no serious efforts visible to undertake restructuring which provides for force and function specialization among the West European states: although France has led to date in space-based reconnaissance, it is actively seeking partners to share more of the cost.

A test of European cooperation in this area will be the coherence of the response to the Euroflag transport aircraft project. The Netherlands has already offered its modest fleet of transport aircraft to a WEU pool, and a very tangible sign of European cooperation would be a joint WEU decision to procure a fleet of transport aircraft which could form a collective asset, to be used, as required, by specific groups of states or even individual states which take on specific intervention activities. Parallel developments could take place in other areas such as space-based reconnaissance, or tanker aircraft. The aim would not be to become independent of the US, but to maximize the number of areas where West Europeans could procure equipment on a scale sufficient to bring down substantially for each state the costs of acquiring and having access to a specific sort of asset. Any such WEU assets could be assigned to NATO for planning purposes, as national units are.

Finally, nuclear force structures are having to be rethought. Progress in arms control discussions, and announcements in NATO and other multilateral communiqués and in unilateral but widely endorsed acts, reflect the considerable consensus. In particular, all of Western Europe has been happy to see the end of INF and tactical nuclear weapons except air-launched systems, and has welcomed the Strategic Arms Reduction Talks agreements which will much reduce the nuclear systems which Russia will have to control. Some trickier issues, where further discussion is needed, include the following:

- Under what circumstances, if any, could British and French nuclear systems provide a deterrent for all of Western Europe, a development seemingly favoured by President Mitterrand?
- Should West Europeans contemplate the threat of the first use of nuclear weapons against a non-nuclear state, especially if that state has used chemical weapons against Western forces or targets?
- Have West Europeans any reasonable voice on the issues of the relative sums devoted by Britain and France to nuclear forces, given the implications for conventional force funding?
- Do Britain and France need nuclear systems other than SLBMs? If so, what sort of systems and why?
- What range of measures should West Europeans take to discourage nuclear proliferation in the wider world and to guard against its consequences should it occur? What attention, and resources, should be devoted to ballistic missile defence?

This range of questions indicates that the medium-term nuclear agenda will be a full one and that the nuclear structures which West Europeans deploy will have major implications for the sort of regional and global orders which they want to promote.

However, the experience of the late 1970s and early 1980s may well make European countries reluctant to bring nuclear issues to the fore. The concern may be less that such issues would bring out major differences among West European governments, and more that nuclear questions divide the politically active groups within Western countries.

Equipment and industry

The Netherlands, Britain and Italy are explicitly committed to the generation of smaller but better-equipped armed forces. However, as Table 4 shows, even in 1993 most European governments were still cutting equipment more than defence budgets overall, so continuing a trend from the late 1980s. In Germany, the proportion of defence spending on equipment has dropped to 12 per cent. Only in France is a major effort visible to sustain defence equipment spending levels, with

Table 4: Fall in real equipment spending in local currency values (%)

Country	Fall between 1989 and 1993
France	n/a
Germany	46
Italy (1989–92 period)	31.8
Netherlands	48
United Kingdom	37.1

Source: Derived from Tables 1 and 5, 'Financial and economic data', op. cit.

over 100 billion francs per year scheduled to be expended in the periods 1992–4 and 1995–7.[6] However, even these amounts may not be adequate to pay for the many major projects to which France remains committed.[7]

Despite these expenditure cuts, and their implications for industry, few signs of national, let alone intergovernmental, debates on the future of defence industrial capabilities can be discerned. At one extreme, France appears anxious to sustain its defence industrial capabilities while, at the other, Germany is happy in principle to run down its defence development and manufacturing and seemingly is thinking on a West European scale. Germany, however, has not yet faced up to abandoning an area of national repute, such as tank manufacture. Britain apparently hopes that UK industrial success in winning MoD and export contracts will be adequate to sustain the UK defence industry in broadly its present form. The Netherlands has implicitly accepted a more European approach by allowing most of its defence industry to be bought by Thomson-CSF and DASA. Italy's defence industry is deeply involved with the wider privatization measures which the government

6. 'Les principaux programmes d'armement coûteront 622 milliards de francs entre 1992 et 1997', *Le Monde*, 25 Nov. 1992.
7. 'Programmation militaire, ambitions de la loi, limites de l'information', *Le débat stratégique*, No. 5, Nov. 1992, from the Centre Interdisciplinaire de Recherches sur la Paix et d'Etudes Stratégiques, Paris.

is pursuing. Thus the sorts of problems addressed by Les Aspin in the US when he was Chairman of the House Armed Services Committee[8] are not yet receiving systematic national or multilateral consideration in Europe. This is despite the assistance which the British and French armed forces needed from their industry in the build-up to the Kuwait war. Insofar as European governments are addressing this issue, they are doing so through the West European Armaments Group in the WEU and the faltering efforts to create a European armaments agency.

Changed defence budgets and changing priorities within defence have had a profound, disruptive effect on collaborative projects. There have been some notable casualties, but most major projects (Eurofighter, NH.90, EH.101, Tiger, Franco-British-Italian frigate and shipborne air defence, Trigat and others) remain in being while facing futures of greater or lesser uncertainty.

Decision-making

As noted above, the aspirations for defence outlined at Maastricht imply cooperation more intense than that achieved in NATO.[9] This raises the question of whether West European governments are sufficiently similar in their governmental structures for such intense cooperation to be achieved without unexpected frictions. Sufficient contrast can be readily identified to raise doubts.

(1) Even in armaments procurement, where cooperative efforts and even successes have a long history, there are problems. All states have identified a 'national armaments director' who also has a representative in his country's NATO delegation, but the executive powers of such people vary from state to state. For

---

8. See, for instance, Rep. Les Aspin, 'Tomorrow's Defense from Today's Industrial Base', address to American Defense Preparedness Association; see also Trevor Taylor, 'West European defence industrial issues for the 1990s', *Defence Economics*, vol. 4, no. 2, 1993, pp. 118–9.
9. See T. Taylor and K. Hayward, *The British Defence Industrial Base*, London, Brasseys, 1989, Ch. 5.

instance, no other West European state has an equivalent in role or influence to the French Délégation Nationale d'Armement.

(2) States vary in the degree to which they seek to operate their armed forces on an integrated basis. Since the mid-1980s Britain has strengthened its central military staff, creating a substantive 'purple' level of military policy-making and decision-making. A commitment to greater inter-service integration ('jointery') was planned for Britain after July 1994. In Italy, by contrast, the services are organized quite separately, and inter-service rivalry is more apparent and coordination more elusive.

(3) In the various states, different patterns of responsibility are apparent among junior ministers and senior officials. Many of them cannot easily identify a single opposite number in ministries in other WEU states.

(4) Parliaments vary in their role and powers with regard to defence. In Germany the Bundestag must approve individual procurement projects (and clearly plays a central role in changing the political/constitutional constraints on German forces). In Britain the Defence Committee and the Public Accounts Committee mainly review aspects of past policy rather than looking forward. The House of Commons rarely debates defence policy although, mainly through the Defence Committee, it examines each year's Defence White Paper. The French National Assembly seldom has a major impact on defence policy.

(5) The methods and degrees of civilian control over the military are not identical. In the Dutch and British defence ministries civilians play a bigger role than in the Germany. Leading military figures have different responsibilities and powers. When the WEU first began to hold regular meetings at Chief of Staff level, there was some British concern that the British representative was being asked to contribute on topics which were not his responsibility.

(6) The relationship of defence ministries to other relevant ministries in a state cannot be overlooked. The Maastricht model sees defence cooperation as closely linked to a common foreign and security policy, which requires a close, coordinated relationship

between the foreign and defence ministries within a state. Such coordination may be limited, especially if they are headed by ministers from different parties in a coalition. European foreign ministries vary in the amount of military/security expertise which their staff possess. Defence ministries vary in their foreign policy expertise. Countries have different patterns of responsibility allocation on 'marginal' subjects such as arms control. Do finance ministries play a similar role with regard to defence subjects, such as the cost-effectiveness of particular procurement plans? West European governments vary in the role they give to other relevant ministries – for instance, it is understood that the Belgian Economics Ministry plays a substantial role in Belgium's procurement choices.

Some of these differences stem from the historical experience of WEU members and their varying concepts of how best to generate defence policy. However, there are certain differences, particularly with regard to Germany, which reflect the fundamental shape of policy. Germany has structured its command and control structures and other aspects of its military hierarchy so that it could not mount major integrated military operations on a national basis.

If European cooperation is to be strengthened, some of the decision-making sources of friction should be eased. All states, for instance, could seek to establish a significant 'purple' element in their armed forces so as to facilitate coordination among the branches on operational and procurement issues. Harmonizing the role of parliaments with regard to defence would be a sensitive and difficult task, yet, particularly at a time when West Europeans are urging East European states to establish civilian, democratic control of defence, it would be useful to explore in detail the advantages and limitations of each model.

Would all these issues matter less if national defence cooperation were to be organized at the international community level rather than at the intergovernmental level? If international staff (in the WEU and/or the EU) were responsible for advancing cooperation, while leaving detailed implementation of agreed measures to governments, would differences in national defence decision-making structures and cultures matter less? Will West European governments need more help from international staffs than they currently envisage in their efforts to cooperate on defence? Clearly these questions may be considered provocative, and politically unwelcome, but they should not be ignored.

Conclusion

This project has identified areas of harmony and friction among the defence and security policies of West European states and, in doing so, has sought to highlight some fundamental questions where further discussion is needed if effective cooperation on specific issues is to be forthcoming. In summary and conclusion, several areas can be stressed as targets for further analysis and discussion.

(1) West Europeans need to develop their basic thinking on global and regional order, on the roles of military intervention, and on the legitimizing basis for such intervention. Recognition needs to be given to the possibility that an intervening force may come under pressure to change role, and the deterrence of conventional aggression through explicit punishment could be given serious consideration.

(2) Unless West Europeans address burden-sharing issues, efforts at intensified cooperation will generate increased friction over the distribution of costs, and over how risks and responsibilities are shared. All major cooperating governments must be seen to be making a reasonable contribution.

(3) There is doubt whether adequate international consultation on force restructuring and cooperation will be forthcoming for West Europeans to develop complementary rapid reaction forces as well as NATO defence units. Collective WEU forces, similar to the NATO AWACs fleet, should be considered in such areas as air transport, strategic reconnaissance and airborne refuelling.

(4) The apparent consensus on many nuclear issues in Western Europe should not disguise the many resource and doctrinal issues which nuclear systems will continue to raise in the future.
(5) Procurement is not losing its priority as an area for cooperation. Governments must give enhanced consideration to the optimum means of procurement in today's circumstances and to the place which defence industrial considerations are to have in future defence policies.
(6) Contrasts in decision-making practices, procedures and cultures will, if not carefully managed and, where possible, harmonized, hinder cooperative efforts in a range of areas.

This volume has tried to point out areas where national policies need to be adjusted to make cooperation possible after the positive prospects for West European cooperation on defence were perhaps exaggerated by the Rome and Maastricht summits. There has consequently been a degree of public disillusionment with how well West Europeans can work together on defence. Yet the potential benefits of such cooperation remain great and the penalties for failure are potentially enormous. West European integration was arguably poorly served by the process leading up to and following the Maastricht Treaty. The 1996 European Intergovernmental Conference, which is committed to addressing a common defence policy, needs major preparatory work on fundamental issues of defence and security thinking.

The chapters in this volume indicate that cooperation among the five states under review is hindered as much by their failure to complete their reviews of post-Cold War security as by any conflicting conclusions they may have reached about it. The predominant situation is that national debates remain under way without any clear end in sight. This, however, leaves some hope for enhanced cooperation, since there are fewer entrenched national positions to be sustained. The 1996 Intergovernmental Conference offers a chance for national thinking to be completed in consultation with allies, rather than in comparative isolation from them.